THE SOUND OF THE SHUTTLE

*Essays on
Cultural Belonging
& Protestantism
in Northern Ireland*

GERALD DAWE

IRISH ACADEMIC PRESS

First published in 2020 by
Irish Academic Press
10 George's Street
Newbridge
Co. Kildare
Ireland
www.iap.ie

9781788551069 (Cloth)
9781788551076 (Kindle)
9781788551083 (Epub)
9781788551090 (PDF)

British Library Cataloguing in Publication Data
An entry can be found on request

Library of Congress Cataloging in Publication Data
An entry can be found on request

Typeset in Sabon LT Std 11/15 pt

Jacket: *Linenscape* by Nevill Johnson (private collection).

Contents

PREFACE

A very different set of essays would be included in *The Sound of the Shuttle* if the writer was starting off today, rather than as the 31-year-old of 1983 when the first of these essays was written. Ireland, north and south, has in so many ways changed greatly for the better and in the process issues other than the focal points covered here would be front and centre in this book. Yet there remain fault lines under the surface and a default position, deeply set within the social mindset of both parts of the island, that there is always someone else to blame for our problems. The sense I have of life in Northern Ireland is of a split society, of ordinary people getting on with their lives as best they can, distanced from any faith in their political leaders. While the institutionalised divisions sketched here have been ameliorated somewhat in the time covered by these essays (1983–2019), there really is no sign of a substantial and lasting change of heart as regards, for instance, integrated education or the balanced outreach workings of what was once known as 'parity of esteem'. The jagged edges of the violent past are still locked within ideological vices.

So selecting this work from four decades, I wanted to bring together various thoughts and responses to some of these 'issues' but in the specific context of Northern Protestantism and the varied and (at times) misunderstood sense of their cultural belonging. This focus can itself be viewed from different perspectives, such as the very title itself, taken from a letter of John Keats during his brief journey through the North in 1818. Think of the sound of the linen mills he heard being the sound of your every day, which would have been the case for many thousands of women and men working in that dominant industry, alongside the many other industries throughout the eastern counties, including the tobacco factories and shipyards of Belfast.

The life of all those workers seems to have been erased from the history books, political discourse and cultural knowledge. But this is not a history book. The bulk of these essays sought to think aloud about a dark time and the way in which significant moral, artistic and cultural matters were being handled in the media, in various publications and in everyday conversations, as well as bearing witness to what was actually happening on the streets of my native city.

The concluding three essays, written in the twenty-first century, take a snapshot of what has happened since the Good Friday Agreement was endorsed by a substantial majority in Ireland in 1998. From the rise and fall of the Celtic Tiger, the peace 'dividend' and the chaos of Brexit – each continues to have a material impact upon the shifting and conflicting sense of cultural identity in present-day Ireland. When Tony Blair stepped out of the Hillsborough hothouse in April 1998 and announced that 'the hand of history' was on the negotiators' collective shoulder, he sounded just a little over-awed: 'A day like today is not a day for sound bites – we can leave those at home – but I feel the hand of history upon our shoulder with respect to this, I really do.'

Now that the twentieth anniversary has come and gone in this Decade of Commemorations, looking back at the *lack* of progress in Northern Ireland, the hand of history seems distinctly less benign and much heavier, if not indeed frozen and gnarled. Government Buildings at Stormont remains locked in a sectarian head count between the unmoving political power bases and the needs of unionism and nationalism. In recalling the habitual trooping up and down the marbled stairs of Stormont and facing the media on the fabled steps outside – to repeat party mantras, or the progress of current 'talks' or, more likely, the lack of it – maybe the heavy hand of Stormont itself should be reviewed. Is the drama of being up there on the Castlereagh hills, under the unswerving reach of Lord Carson's accusatory arm and pointing finger, informing certain attitudes of uncompromising self-importance? Is it even appropriate for such an imposing building to dominate the parliamentary landscape of a post-industrial democracy in twenty-first-century Western Europe, a society that should be caring for all its people's welfare (health, housing, education) by looking forward much more, and not less? Is it time to rethink the physical architecture of Northern Ireland's governing institution alongside the other legacy issues, in an effort to bring some fresh thinking into the equation? Why not think about taking all those (absent) elected representatives, their staffs and civil service and relocate them in a custom-built, fit-for-purpose modern building on the ground level with the rest of the citizens? Just think what initiating a project that could turn out to be for an up and coming generation of architects, builders and craftsmen and -women and the boost it could provide for the local economy. There has to be a suitable site within the spectacular lough shore that carries both connectivity and positive historical resonances.

And as for Stormont? For the splendid grounds, a People's Park for music, gardens, you name it; for the building, an enterprise, digital and innovation academy. Foregrounded within those corridors of power and former party rooms, create a living archival testament to the hundreds of thousands of ordinary men and women who worked across the province in the linen, farming, engineering, manufacturing industries and mills by which the North was globally recognised throughout the late nineteenth and twentieth centuries. And also provide a portrait of Northern society for all those hundreds of thousands who had to leave to find work and a life for themselves elsewhere. Could that work? Would that not be a good way of sign-posting a really better future and even perhaps educating, away from the politically driven stereotypes addressed in part in this collection of essays, many of the present-day politicians in the social and economic history of their own place; where they actually live? Some might regard such an idea as anathema and another seditious diminution of the cultural past of unionism. But maybe, instead, such an imaginative move could secure a different kind of united future to include all the strands of Northern Irish society. For, by its very impressive physical location, Stormont and the weight that goes with it, might benefit from a new lease of creative life; of being reimagined and culturally releasing. In so doing, the carousel of 'History' which we have trailed behind for so long, and with such unproductive results, could be sidestepped. Who can say? A passing thought.

In recent years one striking feature of Northern Irish society has been the prominence and growing recognition of women writers from various parts of the province such as Marie Jones, Wendy Erskine, Rosemary Jenkinson, Lucy Caldwell, Jan Carson, Anna Burns and Stacy Gregg, among many others, as well as cultural commentators and analysts. Unquestionably the 33-year-old writer today would be responding to a whole range of other concerns such as the role of marginalised or migrant communities, which are merely shaded in here as a kind of analogue from an earlier time that might prove instructive (or indeed may not). The essays that follow do not cover this opening ground; nor do they pretend to hold any answers or put forward any simple solutions to the questions they raise about cultural belonging, while illustrating what it means, or has been made to mean, in the closing decades of the twentieth and the first decades of the twenty-first centuries. The intention behind *The Sound of the Shuttle* is to bring into critical focus the experiences, beliefs and achievements of an (at times) much maligned and often misread community generally referred to as Northern protestants but whose inner world is characterised by much difference, dispute and a healthy sense of independence; values of a stoical temperament from which we all might learn a thing or two.

Gerald Dawe
Belfast, November 2019

The modes of pain and pleasure,
These were things to treasure
When times changed and your kind broke camp.

Derek Mahon, 'Death and the Sun'

In memory of Aodan MacPoilin
1948–2016

CHAPTER ONE

FALSE FACES

In her *Irish Times* review of Seamus Heaney's poem-pamphlet *An Open Letter* (1983), Eavan Boland seems both cautious and uncertain about what it and the other Field Day pamphlets stand for:

> A new Ulster nationalism is not my idea of what Irish poetry needs, but I would be quite willing to lay aside this prejudice if the new nationalism contained all the voices, all the fragments, all the dualities and ambiguities of reference; but it doesn't. Judging by the ... pamphlets here in front of me, this is green nationalism and divided culture. 'Whatever we mean by the Irish situation,' writes Derek Mahon, 'the shipyards of Belfast are no less a part of it than a country town in the Gaeltacht.' Would that this were true; or, at least, would that it were real.

An influential member of Field Day's board, Seamus Deane, is clearly conscious of this absent voice when he talks about breaking down stereotypes:

> by making people have the confidence that each of us has a culture that's not going to disappear if it comes in contact with the other. But it's a kind of confidence severely lacking in Unionists, which is why they're so neurotically defensive. That's the problem with Field Day. It's no good just performing our plays and selling pamphlets to people we know. There's no point in continuing unless we can get through to Unionists.

But there is another important point to be made here. It is unclear what this absent voice 'is' and whether there is, in realisable terms, a culture that can be defined as 'Protestant' and unionist. It depends, of course, on how one defines culture but, taking that term in its widest sense, it is fair to say that the Protestant/unionist sense of self derives its meaning (and is 'neurotically defensive' for this very reason) from the fact of its being *undefined*, imaginatively and historically.

The famed inarticulateness, the Ulster that says *No!*, is, after all, a perfectly legitimate right to silence. In a way, the Protestant/unionist culture has no image of itself and consequently accepts those stereotypes which have been created for *political* purposes, be that within Northern Ireland or from London or

Dublin. Stereotypes that are believed in. An important step would therefore be to begin a process of critical definition, if only to reveal the illegitimacy of those terms of reference and to establish new, imaginative ones.

Yet, in dealing with 'Anglo-Irish attitudes', Declan Kiberd addresses himself variously to 'British liberals', 'British writers' and 'English liberals', the very dependency that the Fifth Province justifiably challenges; as he does elsewhere in his pamphlet when he criticises those, such as F.S.L. Lyons, who have received 'praises and prizes' from the English. However, it 'is certainly time', writes Kiberd, 'that British intellectuals applied themselves to a critical analysis of unionism, what it represents, and what it is doing to Britain as a whole'. 'British writers' must 'apply themselves to the study of Ulster Unionism'; English intellectuals have also virtually excluded 'any informed assessment of the deeper meanings of Ulster Unionism'.

Writers and critics in Ireland should indeed consider the 'deeper meanings', not simply of Ulster unionism, but of the entirety of 'Protestant' experience in the North and the common ground Northerners share, irrespective of religion, *as Northerners*. But if, as Declan Kiberd suggests, 'in modern Ulster men's emotions have been ruled not so much by culture as by cash', then the solution will lie in that direction and the 'full understanding of the situation in Ireland today' resolved on that score, whatever about the current intellectual fuss.

But the unverifiability of so much talk about 'identity' springs from a severance from common experience and *its* established terms of negative feeling – hatred, anger, insecurity, bigotry and fear – being sympathetically and imaginatively absorbed. These feelings are fed by particularly virulent forms of supremacy which are themselves reliant upon political and social power-structures throughout the entire country. Only in the North have these become a matter of life and death and they pervade every aspect of contention. It is these terms and their institutionalised structures that will have to be transformed, from the inside, while the dependencies they ritualise will have to be understood and rewritten, before the simple human and ideological barriers to unity are breached in a positive and lasting way.

One notes an implicit interpretation of history as if it were a machine (or monster) which, partially of its own making, but mainly of English making, conscribes 'the Irish' to a world of thought detached from independent action (or creation). 'History' is populated by brutalised marionettes who continue to dominate the way we think and the way we imagine we feel. But the creative and critical dislocation that takes place as a result of the situation does not illuminate the emotional and subjective bonds that keep both sides in the Northern community locked in what has been described by Thomas Kilroy as 'a struggle for the irretrievable'. It is this struggle which has most often been dealt with at the level of self-fulfilling ideas; otherwise, as Richard Kearney remarks in *Myth and Motherland*, it is feared that 'we capitulate to the mindless conformism of fact'. But facts are not mindless and they dominate only when we perceive them abstractly; cascading into vicious cycles, they are seen as unfit for our solving preconceptions. Up close, fixed in the imagination and in historical reason, they have all the energy, often destructive, of life, its power struggles and their moral and political consequences.

History is not to 'blame', but people, and the way the two have drifted apart into exclusive orthodoxies. That is the problem: the human complexity. But when ideas get caught up with only themselves and loosen their moorings in personal experience and historical reality, despite the intention of their being addressed to present social and political conditions, then that critical dialectic has been broken and it is the intellectual process that fossilises, not the world these ideas are intended to change.

There is a conviction which influences much of the discussion about 'identity' that a fundamental unity actually underlies Irish culture if only the people could (or would) see it. Whatever about the political manipulation of this ideal and the conflicting forms it takes, it must be time for writers and critics to explore all the shades of its creative viability.

In saying this, I am not suggesting, as some may, imitating Johnson's anti-Berkeleyan boot against the boulder, that on the rock of one million Protestants thy dreams will perish. Such attitudes betray intolerance and a fear of change. Rather, I am saying that a radical shift of attention is needed. For, in a way, the Protestants of Northern Ireland are peripheral since the critical focus of definition does not *involve* them. They are, and have always been, a belligerent and beleaguered third party, reacting to the various realignments that have taken place between the dominant two of 'Ireland' and 'England' so that, no matter what 'solution' is arrived at they will, more than likely, remain outside it, against the current. They are, though, symbols of a much deeper malaise in the entire island since it no longer has (if it ever had) a cultural *unity*.

By their very existence, along with so much else of contemporary and historical experience which is either left out of the picture or modishly caricatured, they threaten such ideals. As a result, they are portrayed as dull, dour and pragmatic – the usual epithets that say as much about 'Northern Protestants' as similar glosses say about the Republic.

Some take glum satisfaction in this situation; others see Northern Protestant intransigence as one example of those historical facts and cultural conditions that need imaginative exploration, not exploitation. This exploitation has led to the oppressive edifice of the Northern Irish state while permitting the deceit of nationalism (and superficial reactions against it) to make fools or victims of us all.

There is no prescriptive answer here. For the response of the individual imagination is born of a need to get through as best it can to whomever cares to listen. The mediating role of the print and broadcasting world is crucial. For example, take *The Irish Reporter*, an important left-of-centre journal, published in

Dublin. In a recent issue, there are photographs of 'Protestants at play'. In one of them a woman, doing a knees-up, shows off her knickers; in the background is an Orange band.

Side on, the title declares, THE PROTESTANTS. The facing page carries a statement from Sinn Féin on its struggle to improve the quality of life of Irish people. There are other articles dealing with post-colonialism but, stuck there in the back pages, is that unrepentant Protestant woman, having a good time.

Subtextually, she is irredeemable in terms of visual messages. The photograph is a covert sign of an intellectual distaste; for this is no folk session – not in the acceptable sense of either word. This is beyond the pale of cultural and political credibility. Like her people, she is as incorrect as the Twelfth bonfire in Tiger's Bay. But *change* the context to an Irish emigrant centre in Manchester and one can imagine the justifiable anger at this anti-feminist, racist exploitation.

Over recent years, intellectual and cultural attitudes have hardened towards Northern Protestants and, particularly, to those who consider the union with Britain to be a personal and emotional lifeline separate from the perceived introversions and hypocrisies of the Catholic country to the south and west.

This hardening or dismissiveness is a reflection of a general switch-off in the Republic to the North itself. The place seems stuck in a groove few in the Republic have much private time for, even if the old historical business of fighting the British has the strange afterlife of graffiti. Similarly, the once assumed dominance of Northern writing – or writers from the North – has meant that southern writers – or writers based in the Republic – have become much less sensitive to what goes on north of the border. Attitudes vary between truculence, indifference, and fatigue about what precisely a writer's attitude should be to the events there and to the nature of the achievement of the writing that has come from writers born there. The reaction to the initial three volumes of *The Field Day Anthology of Irish Writing* was *in part* a reaction against the Northern-ness of its declared political and cultural concerns, primarily with national identity.

Sensibilities were already geared to attack Field Day and the protracted gestation of its anthological statement on Irish writing. Field Day had, by the end of the 1980s, started to look out of step with cultural and political issues in the Republic – questions about private morality and public corruption, the scandals of emigration and commercial greed – and, as we all now know, the fundamental sea change that took place in the self-perception of women in Irish society.

Yet it is a curious feature of the anthology itself that it shares a 'pan-Irish' uncertainty when addressing the work, within its own political ambit, of writers from the Northern Protestant background. It is a feature on which Damian Smyth jumped in his condemnation of what he saw as the monolithic dogmatism of Field Day's nationalism: 'What cannot be totalised is left out, and the intellectual ethnic-cleansing which sees the absence of the Rhyming Weavers is only slightly less crude in the treatment of the user-friendly Prods of the nationalist discourse'.

Whether or not the absence of the Rhyming Weavers constitutes a capital offence *artistically* is open to question, but on historical grounds the omission is regrettable. The failure to select a just sample of women's writing was, however, inexcusable. As for the 'user-friendly Prods', it is instructive to see the manner in which two of them are described in the anthology.

It has to be said that the headnotes in the anthology vary from the almost apocalyptic eagerness with which John Montague casts himself 'at times' – 'unashamedly in the bardic role of spokesperson for the tribe' – to the subdued etiquette of Michael Longley's 'self-effacing courtesy, his dry good humour'. Longley is, however, inexplicably defined in terms of the 'semi-detached suburban muse of Philip Larkin and ... British post-modernism, as is manifest in his homage to L.S. Lowry'. There is in this summary absolutely no accounting for the surreal, the love lyrics, the bizarre and the classical in Longley, all of which coalesce to make a poetry constitutionally different from the despairing symbolism of Philip Larkin. Longley is also paired with Mahon in a Siamese-twinning of cultural aspiration whereby both poets are taken to represent 'a strand of Ulster that identifies itself as British and asserts its rights to the English lyric'.

Mahon is 'The most underrated Irish poet of the century' – underrated by *whom*? – and the ontological frame of being a 'post-holocaust poet' is hedged in the following terms as one who '*may yet* prove to be the most durable talent of his generation. He writes not just of, but for, posterities' [my italics]. These uncertainties suggest the wide intellectual instability when it comes to examining the cultural and literary issues of Northern Protestantism.

Longley is conscribed to history as an Irish Larkin, while Mahon exists in a futuristic critical limbo. The significance of this unease plays across the cultural and political life of Ireland. It moderates from good-humoured banter and wit, perplexity and arrogance to bewilderment and contempt, with an average mean in sorrow, bemusement and superiority complexes all around. 'Protestants' are considered 'unionists' (or, more fashionably, 'neo unionists') unless they publicly declare to the contrary and seek asylum in 'Irish Literature'. Failure to do so unsettles the kind of cultural agendas that the media, publishing and academic worlds rely upon, both in Ireland and abroad.

In an interview in *The Irish Times* on the occasion of being awarded the Whitbread Prize for his collection *Gorse Fires*, Michael Longley remarked on the selection from his work in *The Field Day Anthology*: 'I object to being embalmed wearing a false face, a mask. I feel diminished and travestied. I had thought of asking to be withdrawn from subsequent editions, but it seemed self-important.'

The sense of not having the freedom to be one's self (to be considered on one's own imaginative ground, so to speak) but inhibited instead by cultural priorities not of one's own making, leads to all sorts of negations and misrepresentations. How could it be, though, that an anthology of this magnitude, such an extraordinary achievement in so very many ways, should end up with a call for it to be pulped and other suggestions of withdrawal? From the convicted 'terrorist' in a prison in the south of Ireland reciting his poems about 'Ireland' that sound little different from the rhetoric of the nineteen-century Young Irelanders, to the designer caricatures surrounding the term 'Northern Protestant', it is tempting to see *all* writing from Ireland as forever folkloric, underpinned by regional or national loyalties and political designs. This is folly, to quote the critic Patrick Wright, because it toys with the idea that politics can be conjured out of cultural roots *at will*. Should this be where we are heading, poetry had better look to its laurels.

1985–93

CHAPTER TWO

TELLING A STORY

I want to discuss a book I edited in 1985 with the literary critic Edna Longley, called *Across a Roaring Hill: The Protestant Imagination in Modern Ireland*. My approach will be mostly informal, drawing upon my own personal story as someone who comes from a Belfast Protestant background and who reacted very negatively against that background until comparatively recently when I started to question, with a more *constructive* critical eye, what I was doing as a poet – namely, exploring my own past, and my family's past, rooted in that specific social background. From this point of view, *Across a Roaring Hill* provided a critical counterpoint to an imaginative quest, both criss-crossing at the very vulnerable, crucial and even deadly intersection between 'region' (based, in my case, in a Protestant Belfast) and 'nation' (British or Irish).

Put simply, *Across a Roaring Hill* was, for me, a gesture to all those anonymous Protestants who saw literature as something alien to them and to what they considered to be their 'way of life'. I wanted to establish that some of Ireland's greatest writers in the twentieth century were, in fact, *Protestant* and that there *was* nothing inherently contradictory about such a state of affairs: a reality to which they had rarely been exposed. In having this door opened to them, the brilliant complexity of literature, might somehow be revealed, irrespective of categories of religion or definitions of place.

It would, in other words, be an ideal critical equation, paralleling what I found myself trying to do in poems: exploring the past, seeking clearly balanced moments of personal and historical tension and coincidences whereby one sees the influences, expectations and beliefs that govern one's own self-image and, by implication, the community's out of which one came.

To what extent was there a 'Protestant imagination' or, more accurately, what creative valence ran between these two terms? This was the basic question which I felt needed some kind of answer. As a poet, I was trying to relate those writers in Ireland who meant something to me with the majority of other writers, not Irish, who were also personally significant. I was thinking of 'tradition' and trying to sort out the question of there being a coherent 'Protestant' literary tradition in which I could sound out my own experience in imaginative and cultural terms.

The answer is, I am convinced, that no such tradition exists in Ireland but, rather, as stated in the introduction to *Across a Roaring Hill*, that there is 'an eradicable consciousness of *difference*, of being defined in and against another culture' which makes, for instance, a 'direct descent in the Protestant line' still discernible, as in 'the evolution of forms and images from Yeats to MacNeice to Mahon'. Yet, like the term 'Anglo-Irish', the notion of a distinctly 'Protestant' literary tradition inevitably calls upon Yeats (or Burke or Swift) as 'the father' and, as W.J. McCormack correctly points out in his *Ascendency and Tradition* (1985): 'Biological metaphors of this kind have an insidious effect in that they generate notions of a legitimising family tree which distinguishes the Anglo-Irish writer from a larger context instead of locating him in it.'

My own personal and social experience resisted such notions of 'a legitimising family tree', seeing instead the disjointed, fragmentary nature of Northern Protestantism. While this background offered people of my age the educational resources to move out into the wider community, it recoiled, for various specific historical factors, economic dependencies and religious susceptibilities, into a state of isolation – defensive and suspicious, constantly vigilant of possible betrayal and 'sell-out'. Belonging to such a tradition was, from the start, a very mixed blessing.

'My people, provided that I have one,' as Franz Kafka remarked; and the 'return' to them is mined with anger and self-consciousness that can prove to be creatively crippling. Yet writers from such a Protestant background in Ireland are, *ipso facto*, more alert to the various undercurrents of meaning which one associates with terms like 'region' and 'nation', since they are never sure of their place in this system of things. They can take little for granted, except by a force of will or assumption. The community out of which they come is characterised by an obstinate silence in which trenchant dignity runs side by side with the triumphalism of the Orange Order or the noxious patronage of the Unionist Party, the twin ruling partners of the Protestant North. If these were 'my people', and they 'were sinking', as the South African novelist André Brink has written in *Mapmakers: Writing in a State of Siege* (1983), 'then it was their own fault, the inevitable retribution for what they themselves had done and allowed to be done'. Coming from such a background catches the writer in a spider's web: the more one tries to draw away, the more entangled one becomes. This is how the situation was described in the introduction to *Across a Roaring Hill*:

> There is a heritage of guilt, repressed, formless and diffuse; and of tribal customs and binding beliefs which individuals – and writers – transgress at their peril: Calvinist cultures expel art from the city's gates, because they fear its power to penetrate communal neurosis – aggravated by such exclusion.

It is a fairly common experience of writers who seek to come to terms with a cultural inheritance, such as this, to have great difficulty coping with its religious bigotry and the prejudice that is itself an irrational protest against the world and evidence of an inability to understand it.

What has happened in Northern Ireland is that, with such worldwide attention, the experience of ordinary people becomes contentious and can be converted easily into cliché and caricature – the processed suffering and recycled grievance, the everlasting 'victim' as much as the deluded superiority of insularity and bigotry. This places an added burden upon the writer and critic to ensure that what he or she writes is meticulously weighed against the political use to which it can be put.

Albert Camus' remark about the 'reserve' of the Breton writer Louis Guilloux, whom he greatly admired, is relevant here since Camus saw this artistic virtue as a way of preventing the writer from 'permitting the misery of others ... to offer a picturesque subject for which the artist alone will not have to pay'. On another level, too, this reserve is an act of fidelity which establishes a self-critical distance rather than a falsely modest style of understatement. It relates not only to one's own politically grounded experience but also to the notion of 'tradition' itself: in my case, to a sanctified corpus of Irish literature in English that stretches from the eighteenth century to the present.

How could such a mythical continuum actually *exist*, given the profound economic, social, political and cultural changes that have happened on this island and, specifically, in that part of it in which I had grown up? It is a contradiction 'between tradition and its material' or, stated crudely, between the past and the present. To call upon W.J. McCormack's excellent *Ascendency and Tradition* again, this contradiction is 'a further statement of the disjunction between an Irish local literature and the European culture into which it cries out for reinsertion'.

In an atmosphere of great uncertainty and frustration, bitterness and hatred, when people turn to literature among other things – as a means of overcoming religious and political divisions – it is difficult to take up that responsibility without, at the same time, running the risk of burdensome self-consciousness or, more importantly, of limiting, by definition, the way literature undermines *every* kind of division, from the 'regional' to the 'national'. On this Jacob's ladder, which rung does one start on? Yet with various poetic voices of 'History' and 'Prophets of the People' being called for, to speak directly out of personal experience appears to be a mute, almost tame, exercise in the flux of what is clearly a time of great tension and change. As the main character, Hans, says in *The Clown*, Heinrich Böll's novel about life in post-war Germany: 'the secret of the terror lay in the little things. To regret big things is child's play – political errors, adultery, murder, anti-Semitism – but who forgives, who understands the little things?' Sticking to a vigorous and exacting sense of what one knows and experiences assumes a kind of austere radicalism but, as so often happens with personal experience, when it becomes *representative* through the prism of literature, it can slide imperceptibly from being treated objectively towards being seen as picturesque and – in due course – imperilled by easy nostalgia.

To give an extreme example of this process: the dwindling battalions of bowler-hatted Orangemen on 12 July are first seen strictly in their native setting but, once they are taken out of that context, they are invariably considered as quaint remnants of a formidably decayed tradition, which are then held up, no longer to ridicule, but to a patronising curiosity. The fate of the theme park. The danger in all this, and one to which I trust *Across a Roaring Hill* was keenly alert, is suggested most cogently by Salman Rushdie in his essay 'Outside the Whale' (1984):

> there can be little doubt that in Britain today, the refurbishment of the Empire's tarnished image is under way. The continuing decline, the growing poverty, and the meanness of spirit of much of Thatcherite Britain, encourages many Britons to turn their eyes nostalgically to the lost hour of their precedence.

It is, of course, the Protestants of 'Northern Ireland', 'Ulster', 'the North' and the 'Six Counties', who are so visibly trapped in the 'lost hour of their precedence', while unemployment grows under the Tory ministers who directly rule the North. This is, then, the immediate social world that *Across a Roaring Hill* came out of and, ironically, returned to when it was launched in

Belfast at the International Association for the Study of Anglo-Irish Literature conference of 1985, which included a trip to Stormont – the delegates being greeted by a Yeatsian anecdote from the then Deputy Secretary of State, Rhodes Boyson.

Given such meshing of literature, culture and politics, it is hardly surprising that, as Brian Friel remarked, 'everything is immediately perceived as political and the artist is burdened instantly with politicisation'. How to deal with politicisation is a question for the individual artist, *but what kind of politics*? is something we could all do with questioning. The trouble is that very often these two distinct, if not separate, issues get mixed up. For instance, in an insightful discussion of the Field Day Company, Joseph McMinn interprets the various critical responses to it as 'concealed political objections' to their 'dissemination of nationalist views of culture': 'Arguing for an apolitical analysis of Irish culture which will be sensible, moderate, rational, unemotional, dispassionate, is to take up a political position without naming it. It is an extension of unionist political values into the cultural area.'

It is unclear precisely *who* is arguing for an apolitical analysis of Irish culture but of all the Heinz varieties of unionism, I have not met one that fits the bill here – sensible, moderate, detached and so on. The only political values that unionism has expressed are immoderation and an entrenched inability to be detached in *any* sense. (Nor, it should be said, is this the sole prerogative of unionism, as anyone will know who witnessed the moral debates in the Republic of Ireland on abortion and divorce.)

Confronting the historical *impasse* which a region called 'the North' is in, where unionism, whether it is liked or not, *is* the political voice of a substantial majority of the people who live there (and who do not want, and will probably violently resist, belonging to a nation called 'Ireland'), there is an obvious imaginative and critical need to explore the experience of this people, their reasons for seeing life as they do and of placing this in the wider context (political, cultural and literary) of the whole country. In other words, to probe and possibly restore the shattered bonds of 'region' and 'nation' at an imaginative level which defines them both, bearing in mind the fact that the so-called question of 'the North' has no reality in isolation but is a part of, and a major critical influence upon, the 'Irish/British' question. It would be ironic, though, if such an aspiration was interpreted politically as propping up unionism, although what *point* there would be in such an exercise I cannot for the life of me imagine.

Considering this relationship of 'region' to be an acknowledgement of diversity and difference within the ambit of 'nation', Seamus Deane, in his *Irish Times* review of *Across a Roaring Hill*, wrote:

> Ireland must give its deference to difference and defer its 'unitary' ambitions. I find this interesting, but would like to have it identified more precisely. Is it a defence of

Unionism cast in cultural terms? Or is it
a plea for the recognition of a diversity
which is in danger of being ignored?

The answer is an emphatic *Yes* to the second question,
as everyone engaged in these issues of 'region' and
'nation' must surely accept and support, or else we
lurch towards some covert or doctrinaire concept
of authoritarian statehood. But against this reason,
Enoch Powell, in his review of the book in *The Times*
(15 August 1985), saw *Across a Roaring Hill* as one in
a line of work 'much petted and encouraged by those,
in Great Britain and elsewhere, who want to bully
the Northern Ireland electorate out of their settled
conviction to remain within the United Kingdom'.
Rather than being a putative *defence* of unionism, the
book is seen as attacking it.

One can see at this stage where the burden of
politicisation, of which Brian Friel speaks, slides into
gyres of rhetoric. The complex ways that human feeling
is enmeshed with cultural affiliation evaporate and the
actual manipulators of political identity (who, after
all, *control* and embody power) get off the hook. What
is more, it treats the experience of others (Northern
Protestants, in this instance) to a further illustration
of the kind of fashionable disdain they have come to
expect and denies that very diversity in Irish life which
demands recognition, if the relationship between
'region' and 'nation' is ever going to be unbloody.

To define and elucidate these different kinds of
experience and ideas is, I think, an essential obligation

if we are ever going to understand adequately the state Ireland is in, never mind realising the one that many of us hope it will become. This is one definite place where the writer has an important role to play, as André Brink suggests, 'of fighting to assert the most positive and creative aspects of his heritage'. And we should not forget all those who, over the years, to quote Christopher Hitchens, have challenged 'their own tribes with criticism, opposition and argument *from within*'. It is important to add here that this imaginative struggle is, as Brink says, also often *against* those who 'can afford to clash with authority because they are basically protected *by* it'.

If there is, as I believe there to be, a world of difference between the experience of Protestant families in the North, their feelings, fears, hopes and ambitions (the stuff one hears so much pious talk about in the Republic) and the *political* use made of them, then the crucial discrimination must be made and maintained between the two sets of experiences and the various economic, social and cultural bonds that keep them bound together.

If this effort at understanding be dubbed 'Unionist', we will have missed another chance to expose the invidious forms of falsehood and violence which oppress people on the small island of Ireland; and have done so because of fashionable intellectual posturing, not out of serious political commitment and work. For it is an effort of knowing the past which requires us, as Peter Gay well knew on the truly horrendous scale of his native Germany, to 'mobilize historical understanding and to make discriminations [which do] not mean to deny or to prettify what has happened'.

Across a Roaring Hill was just a small part of the process whereby prevailing mythologies and the ways they are, in turn, transformed into art, are opened up and brought into the light of day. It is a first step: exploratory and, within its limits, diverse and speculative. As this process comes under an imaginatively sustained criticism, everything is up for grabs – not just a monolithic 'Irish' literary tradition, but the very notion of 'tradition' itself, the language used to discuss these things and our *working through* the inherited ways of seeing them both. This is the truly radical challenge that the present offers; not painting ourselves back into a corner which so often seems to be the case in Ireland.

The relationship between a 'Protestant' or 'Catholic', 'nationalist' or 'unionist' experience is only one, if presently dominant, cultural and political distinction. Like all labels, they bear the marks of prejudice from which few are free. One has to take into account, however, entire tracks of historical and contemporary experience that are of vital significance in Ireland today – 'loyalty' and the question of 'belonging', such as that considered in Thomas Kilroy's play *Double Cross*, or the force field of community and the individual's own complicated place within it which John McGahern has explored to such telling effect in, for example, *High Ground* – to say nothing about the explosion of women's writing in Ireland in recent times.

These are issues that come readily to my own mind since I have an abiding interest in them as a writer, but they underpin the present and are bound to have serious implications for the kind of literature (and politics) that many want to see taking over from the current conventions and official dogmas. I think this is the point behind Seamus Deane's close reading of *Across a Roaring Hill* when, in singling out Bridget O'Toole's essay on Jennifer Johnston, Elizabeth Bowen and Molly Keane, he writes:

> a sentence from Elizabeth Bowen ... might have been this volume's epigraph and ... has its application, economic and cultural, for Protestants and Catholics: 'We have everything to dread from the dispossessed'. It is in dispossession that the hurt, Protestant and Catholic, lies.

Material deprivation and cultural dispossession are indeed fundamental 'themes', since they are the common inheritance of so many Irish men and women. It would be a shame if this fact was lost sight of and turned, on the lathe of dogma, into an obligatory truth from which those who actually *live it out* can find no real imaginative release or critical yet sympathetic distance. As Terence Brown eloquently put it in his Field Day pamphlet, *The Whole Protestant Community: The Making of a Historical Myth*:

> A people who have known resistance as well as dissent, rebellion, dispute, religious

enthusiasm in the midst of rural and urban deprivation, have an interesting story to tell themselves – one of essential homelessness, dependency, anxiety, obdurate fantasising, sacrifices in the name of liberty, villainous political opportunism, moments of idealistic aspiration. And in the telling of it they may come to realise at last where they are most at home and with whom they share that home.

The colloquial 'Tell us a story' goes far beyond a child's need for reassurance – it opens out the ground of imaginative possibility as well. What we are seeing in Ireland today is a clash between the traditional ways of perceiving these possibilities and the need to bypass the politics which stunts them. The writer is caught – appropriately enough – in the middle.

1986

CHAPTER THREE

ARMIES OF THE NIGHT

I

When Mrs Thatcher, the then prime minister of Great Britain and Northern Ireland, met two Irish clerics, Cardinal Ó Fiaich and Bishop James Lennon, on 1 July 1981 at Downing Street, she was, according to David Beresford,

> waiting for them at the top of the stairs, on the first-floor landing, and gushed a welcome ... They started with the usual pleasantries, but quickly moved onto the prison issue.
>
> 'Will someone please tell me why they are on hunger strike?' asked the Prime Minister. 'I have asked so many people. Is it to prove their virility?'

Two months earlier, following the death of Bobby Sands, Francis Hughes had died on hunger strike, and in the month of August Tom McIlwee was also to die. Hughes and McIlwee were cousins, in their mid-twenties, born within a year of each other (1956 and 1957), from Bellaghy, County Derry. They were buried together, 'in a new section of the cemetery at St. Mary's Church':

> Their tombstone is inscribed in Irish which Tom – battling to learn the language even as he was dying – would have particularly appreciated. And Frank would have liked the wording: 'Among the warriors of the Gael may his soul rest'.

David Beresford's *Ten Men Dead* is full of such chilling contrasts. How is it possible, one asks, for two islands so physically, economically, culturally and socially close as Britain and Ireland, to be so grotesquely divided. *History and language*?

In his collection of essays, *Less Than One*, Joseph Brodsky often returns to the inextricable mesh of expression and experience. Discussing Andrei Platonov, he sees the Russian novelist as 'a millenarian writer if only because he attacks the very carrier of millenarian sensibility in Russian society: the language itself – or, to put it in a more graspable fashion, the revolutionary eschatology embedded in the language'. Brodsky goes on to define the roots of Russian millenarianism in the following terms:

> On the mental horizon of every millenarian movement there is always a version of a

New Jerusalem, the proximity to which is determined by the intensity of sentiment. The idea of God's city being within reach is in direct proportion to the religious fervour in which the entire journey originates. The variations on this theme include also a change of the entire world order, and a vague, but all the more appealing because of that, notion of a new time, in terms of both chronology and quality. (Naturally, transgressions committed in the name of getting to a New Jerusalem fast are justified by the beauty of the destination.) When such a movement succeeds, it results in a new creed. If it fails, then, with the passage of time and the spread of literacy, it degenerates into utopias, to peter out completely in the dry sands of political science and the pages of science fiction. However, there are several things that may somewhat rekindle soot-covered embers. It's either severe oppression of the population, a real, most likely military peril, a sweeping epidemic, or some substantial chronological event, like the end of a millennium or the beginning of a new century.

Somewhat later in the same essay, 'Catastrophes in the Air', Brodsky remarks that the first casualty of any discourse about utopia – desired or attained – is grammar; for language, unable to keep with this line of thought, begins to gasp in the subjunctive mood and starts to gravitate toward categories and constructions of a rather timeless denomination. As a consequence of this, the ground starts to slip out from under even the simplest nouns, and they gradually get enveloped in an aura of arbitrariness.

Platonov, according to Brodsky, 'was able to reveal a self-destructive eschatological element within the language itself, and that, in turn, was of extremely revealing consequences to the revolutionary eschatology with which history supplied him as the subject matter'.

The image of Platonov which Brodsky presents, in contrast to Kafka, Joyce or Beckett, 'who narrate quite natural tragedies of their *alter egos*', itself verges on the apocalyptic:

Platonov speaks of a nation which in a sense has become the victim of its own language ... he tells a story about this very language, which turns out to be capable of generating a fictitious world, and then falls into grammatical dependence on it.

The ten Republican paramilitaries who died on hunger strike in 1981 were mostly from old country families.

Three were Belfast men and one was from Derry city. The oldest of them was born in 1951 and the youngest in 1957. With remission, nine of the ten would have been out of Long Kesh in 1987. *Ten Men Dead* moves with close and careful reconstruction through the awful months when the prisoners inside the prison fought off attempts at 'criminalisation'. 'Instead of pulling out, Britain dug in even deeper, reimposing direct rule after a brief experiment in power-sharing and devising the three-prong strategy: Ulsterisation, normalisation and criminalisation – which found one form of physical expression in the building of the H-Blocks.' The criminalisation policy, according to Beresford, sought to deny

> a belief held dear by Republican Ireland
> – that husbands, wives, boyfriends,
> girlfriends, parents, grandparents and
> great-grandparents who had suffered and
> died for Irish independence had done so in
> the high cause of patriotism.

As Terence MacSwiney, Lord Mayor of Cork, had put it in his inaugural speech (1920): 'the contest on our side is not one of rivalry or vengeance, but of endurance. It is not those who can inflict the most, but those that can suffer the most who will conquer.' And, in an essay, MacSwiney hailed 'the day when the consciousness of the country will be electrified with a great deed or a great sacrifice and the multitude will break from lethargy or prejudice and march with a shout for freedom a true, a brave and a beautiful sense'.

First by refusing to wear uniforms, then through the 'blanket' protest, the 'no wash' and the 'dirty' protests, the Long Kesh prisoners were finally cornered, through failure to achieve their basic objectives ('the five demands') which were for recognition of their political status. Rather than ending the blanket protest, abandoning the hunger strike and organising themselves very much as the British had done in prisoner of war camps during World War II, the Republican prisoners were, as Beresford states, drawn back to MacSwiney and those who endure the most.

> It was not a practical approach [one of the prisoners maintained] ... you came out of it with moral superiority, but the Movement already has that ... and so did not need to do it. What the prisoners had to do was win the battle and in order to do that they needed to be more flexible, to adopt a two-pronged approach – try to destroy the system by working within it while at the same time standing outside it.

The harking back to previous generations and times so totally different from the present gives a kind of hallucinatory quality to the story. The isolation of the Provo leadership 'living in something of a political cocoon' is compounded by the innocence of the hunger-strikers. Hardened by injustice, risk, guilt and insularity, their expectations of life were heavily guarded from childhood by sentinels of nationalist piety. That religious force which Father Denis Faul refers to when blaming churchmen 'in a way for what happened: saying that, after all, they taught people to imitate Christ, so the Church can hardly complain when they go out and do just that' blends with the established, traditionalist cultural imperatives of the Irish language and the GAA to reinforce the utopianism instilled in the Catholic youth of Northern Ireland. When this confronts a force, state or system totally hostile to such things, redress seems to follow the logic of utopianism itself. The future (a United Ireland) matters more than the present (a divided province). So one gives oneself literally to posterity – 'those that *can* suffer most ... *will* conquer'. The grammatical dependence is already there; the prejudice, bigotry and oppression hang like a cloud constantly in the background. A new 'pure' world can be generated in its place:

> Hunger-striking, when taken to the death, has a sublime quality about it; in conjunction with terrorism it offers a consummation of murder and self-sacrifice which in a sense can legitimise the violence which precedes and follows it. If after killing or sharing in a conspiracy to kill – for a cause one shows oneself willing to

die for the same cause, a value is adduced
which is higher than that of life itself. But
the obverse is also true: failure to die can
discredit the cause. To scream for mercy at
the foot of the gallows – or nod at the saline
drip as kidneys and eyes collapse and the
doctor warns of irreversible damage – is
to affirm that there is no higher value than
life and none worthy of condemnation
than those who take it.

Inevitably, David Beresford's book makes one ask:
what did these young men die for? But no answer
presents itself. Instead, Beresford's strict grasp of
narrative falters in the concluding pages and blurs
into a self-enfolding, fatalistic assumption that Irish
history is duty-bound to repeat itself *ad infinitum*.
The hunger-strikers 'died for a cause far more ancient
than the grey walls of Long Kesh prison'. But people
do not die on hunger strike for a cause because it is
old. Perplexed by the precise reasons and the political
significance of whatever they may be, Beresford inserts
clichés: 'the age-old struggle', 'time immemorial', the
'centuries-old struggle' – all subsumed in the stretched
theatrical context of W.B. Yeats' play *The King's
Threshold*:

When I and these are dead
We should be carried to some windy hill
To lie there with uncovered face awhile

> That mankind and that leper there may
> know
> Dead faces laugh. King! King! Dead faces
> laugh.

But the point of *The King's Threshold* is lost: Seanchan, the poet, stands up for poetry, the imagination, and refuses to become a mere crony of King Guaire and his council-chamber.

At times, *Ten Men Dead* reads like the literature the prisoners were themselves reading: Kipling, Wilde and Eilís Dillon. Bobby Sands makes a special request:

> I was wondering ... that out of the goodness of all yer hearts you could get me one miserly book and try to leave it in: the *Poems of Ethna Carberry* – cissy. That's really all I want, last request as they say. Some ask for cigarettes, others for blindfolds, yer man asks for poetry.

In some way that I have not been able to define, the lives of these ten men were surrounded by a kind of estranged ether, an emotional and intellectual current no longer earthed to the core realities of Ireland as it is today. Unquestionably, they knew and had unforgettable first-hand experience of sectarianism and militarism. Equally, the cultural idealism that has emerged out of this situation has brought with it a sense of dignity long denied by the political state of Northern Ireland. It is, though, the complex contradiction which manifests itself through their double life, as bombers and murderers and as freedom-fighters and Irish soldiers, which defeats me. It seems fuelled by the early tragic world of Irish peasants that was converted into the poetic stock of Yeats' revivalist prose and ballads of the late nineteenth century. It defies any bearing to the social and cultural reality of the country as a whole, and even less to the deprivation of Belfast. Rhetoric is a pitiless word when lives are laid on the line: 'We re-confirm and pledge "our" full confidence and support to you and march on with you to the Irish Socialist Republic.'

If the 'ten men dead' were victims of language, then it is because of a myth that nationalism sows in the heart. Achievements in the Republic – of a welfare system, an adequate education, jobs and houses for all; social freedom and cultural independence; confidence and outwardness – are historically vulnerable. Militant nostalgia is no challenge in this context. As Salman Rushdie remarked, the real challenge is to discover 'that one's entire picture of the world is false, and not only false but based upon a monstrosity. What a task for any individual: the reconstruction of reality from rubble.' In a way, the dominant forces of nationalism have brought little to the ordinary people but the sweet, breathless banality of 'Is it to prove their virility?' or the shattered wrecks of men, 'prison-pale skin stretched across paradoxically young skull-like faces' with what Bobby Sands had once described as 'that awful stare, of the pierced, or glazed eyes'.

1987

II

Calling someone a monster does not make him more guilty; it makes him less so by classing him with beasts and devils.

Mary McCarthy, *The Hue and Cry*

The Shankill Butchers by Martin Dillon is a harrowing book. It deals with a ghastly period in the sickly underworld of Belfast's sectarian life which anyone who lived through that time in the 1970s, who knows the geography of these outrages and the people who were tortured and did the torturing, will naturally want to forget. The newspaper reports of the trials of these men – who methodically and determinedly brutalised, dehumanised and slaughtered their way through the mid-1970s, leaving in their wake some thirty working-class Catholics and Protestants dead – make for terrifyingly grim reading. But why, one has to ask, has this Belfast world of violence, pathological hatred, squalid introversion and appalling narrow-mindedness not been exposed before? How can the miserable lives of bigots seek the darkness of anonymity and get away with it?

I was reminded of these questions constantly when reading Martin Dillon's brave book. It must have been a heart-rending job to absorb into himself the disgraceful acts of the Shankill butchers and the arbitrariness with which their victims were picked. All that mattered was 'to get a Taig'. But that act alone was earthed, as Dillon so rightly says, in an environment 'fuelled by extreme prejudice ... developed since childhood and which found an outlet in acts so violent that they could only have been committed by a psychopath'. In linking the psychopathology of these murderers to the prejudice of Northern Irish society and, in particular, of Belfast, Martin Dillon has established a shatteringly simple truth about that society. Namely, the *cost* to it of being a self-divided society, based upon intolerance and ignorance; a condition that may lead eventually towards disintegration and collapse, if not of 'the State' – which looks remarkably resilient – then of 'the People'.

Ironically, this condition has very little to do with politics since real political discussion in the North is limited. What clusters around the religious distinction between Protestant and Catholic cultures is a desperate longing for identity in a society that lacks a *common* one.

When the Provos destroyed Belfast with their civilian-targeted bombs, and the UVF and UDA assassinated Catholics and their own 'traitors', the corruption of Belfast's sectarian past spilled onto the streets again. As Dillon writes:

> Northern Ireland has a society where prejudice is so deeply rooted that extermination rather than derision is the likely outcome when nothing is done to erode it. In most instances the victims of prejudice are not the combatants but the innocent. It is difficult, of course, to eradicate prejudice but serious and

concerted attempts should have been
made to replace it with tolerance and more
positive attitudes within the churches and
the educational system.

These minimal recommendations were studiously
avoided in the 1950s and '60s. By the end of that
decade it was too late. The jails are now packed with the
perpetrators of some of the worst murders committed
by young men to their fellow citizens in these islands.
As Dillon points out, the Shankill Butchers were mass
murderers but given the extent of prejudice 'which is
endemic in Northern Ireland there was an inevitability
that it would end up in "extermination"'.

This is precisely what the 1970s and '80s in
Northern Ireland became: a moral and psychic
landscape traversed by men and women dedicated to
violence. There are no ifs and buts about this fact yet,
for some reason, we all in Ireland try to sidestep this
basic truth. Where are the books *about* violence and
recent history; sectarianism; the struggle against both;
the make-up and reality of paramilitary life?

We live in a society that has methodically refused,
institutionally, culturally and politically, to own up
to lassitude and the acceptance of violence as a means
of effecting change. Dillon casts light on the last two
decades of life in the North and the way this experience
is channelled through ideals and assumptions rarely in
touch with human reality.

'While I was in [Long Kesh] Gerry Adams
advocated the use of explosives as a means of stepping

up the IRA campaign. I interpreted that to mean car bombs which later wrecked Belfast and caused untold casualties in 1972 and 1973', one informant is quoted as saying in Dillon's book, putting in context what was unleashed by the Shankill Butchers a little later. As Dillon says in his conclusion, 'Terrorists are impervious to expressions of morality even when such expressions are part of a public disavowal of violence.' His hope is that his book will 'at least have created the basis for debate about the nature of prejudice'.

The paramilitaries who populate Dillon's book and the real world outside *their* existence, are fed by, and in turn feed, the hunger of a people whose lives are distorted in a twisted society. The transcendence of that world takes the form of dominating it through violence, brash displays of power; acting, as Belfast jargon has it, 'the big man'. When this act turns into the phantasmagoria of literal control over the life and death of an individual, a street, a district, the carved-up compass of a society, anything can happen. In such delusions the human form, like the victims cut and tortured by the Shankill Butchers or the incinerated remains of the people caught up in the La Mon bombing, is despised as weak and flawed. Mistakes become tactical errors. The individual gets in the way. There are, simply, no problems, except logistics. People, in a perverse logic, do not count.

Martin Dillon's book illustrates the grim reality of such fantasy. For the Butchers, most of whom are still behind bars, their world really was, on this telling, a despicable place. Their dependencies were real enough:

drink, violence as a way of life, each other; cocooned from outsiders who might prey upon them and in some way show them up – the peculiarly Northern fear of being, not captured, but 'found out'. This fear breaks through, finally, when they are apprehended and in custody: under the light of day, their defences crumble. Reality breaks through; there is no ideological or mental barrier between the means and ends of what was done. For there is no political protection or psychological drilling capable of withstanding the reality of their crimes against humanity. One of them, who had been involved in particularly gruesome throat-cuttings, broke down, cried and said: 'My head's away with it.' He also asked himself if he was 'wise'.

Another of the gang, after sentencing, ended up in prison close by the Provisional IRA leader Brendan Hughes, who remarked of the UVF man:

> He talked a lot to me and was intrigued to know about republicanism. I felt that suddenly here was a guy who had been involved in killing a lot of people and who had probably mouthed political slogans but never understood them … The one thing which struck me about [the man] was his need to have even someone like me as a friend. He demonstrated a curious loyalty to me. …

Whatever the presumption of moral supremacy here ('a guy who had been involved in killing a lot of people' and 'probably mouthed political slogans but never understood them' is how a lot of people would see IRA activists), the dependency and tension revealed in these extracts bear directly upon the appalling contrast between the dreamlike, insulated state and the 'outside' reality of the paramilitary world. Between these extremes, like an obsessive metronome, the activist is eventually drawn back and forth, with increasingly narrow odds on his or her personal survival but also a decreasing likelihood of their seeing actual *political* change as a direct result of their actions. All that matters, all that happens, is the 'war', the 'struggle', call it what you will.

This might well be the lesson of *The Shankill Butchers*: that violence does not make anything really change. The victim is buried alongside the torturer; the bomber with the bombed. The terrible misreading inside the various factions of political possibility which took place in the North during the 1970s and '80s led only to a further twist in the downward spiral of self-defeating violence and now, twenty odd years down the road, one has to ask: what has really changed and what will be the difference when we reach the twenty-fifth anniversary of 'the Troubles'?

What *The Shankill Butchers* also proves is that, lacking a true sense of political and cultural well-being, split against itself, denied any wider vision from either school or church, the North has teetered from one subdued crisis to another. Those who ruled it, either before or since partition, had very little interest in what went on in the streets and avenues of Belfast.

Martin Dillon's *The Shankill Butchers* is fearsome. It will not be palatable to those commentators in the British and US press who like their history neat and uncomplicated by vile reality. The book will also pierce the banal coverage of much of the Republic's media, bored and bothered as they are by 'Europe' and the soft-centred nationalism of their own gradually disappearing past.

I can only think of those streets where I grew up and walked with girlfriends, going home after dances in town, or parties, without a care in the world, and realise how that time will never come back to those who were so cruelly torn from this life by men and women who lived just a few streets away. It will take a huge leap of imagination before this dammed-up tragedy is released, understood and overcome by all those who physically and morally want to reconstitute the meaning of home.

1990

CHAPTER FOUR

ANECDOTES OVER A JAR

I

I was in Holland in 1981 with Richard Murphy, on a reading tour, and in Amsterdam we were separately interviewed. The keen radio personality wanted me to talk about 'violence' and 'political repression' and later on, in a taxi, I heard my own voice, with estranged *gravitas*, struggling to answer him. It was obvious that the good Dutch radio man had clear ideas about Ireland and wanted to have them confirmed in double-quick time before moving on to the next item – William Burroughs, who was sitting in a marble-like pool of silence, cane in hand and Trilby hat.

It was my first experience of the weight of assumption and expectation that bears upon the two words 'Irish poet'. Five years later, in a packed hotel in Sydney, for the city's Poetry Festival, the sign on the door revealed an 'Irish Poet' reading along with Les Murray and Tom Murphy. Through the steamy night, lots of people milled in and out but, halfway through my stint, a (drunken) voice came from the back of the hall: 'You're not following in the footsteps of Heaney.' This question, complaint or statement (I was never sure which) was patently true since I was reading my own poems and they have little to do with Seamus Heaney's. But I understood what the man meant.

Probably an expatriate, here he was amongst a mixed bunch of 'ex-pats' of all kinds and on stage was this poet, from Ireland mark you, reading poems *not* about the Ireland he knew, or thought he knew: what Seán O'Faoláin called the 'traditional life-concept'. And, if you weren't insulted, the poet was actually talking about Edward Carson, for Christ's sake, and little towns in the North of which no one had ever heard. What he heard simply did not *fit*. And he was having none of it.

Another quirky illustration might indicate the weight of expectation that lies upon this notion of the Irish poet, whether at home or abroad. It is a fascinating subject in itself since critics of writing from Ireland have rarely touched upon its powerful influence, particularly via the United States.

I met an European literary journalist accompanied by an avid Irish intellectual trend-spotter. In the brief exchange, I was asked for an opinion on several questions: about 'the loss of Irish', colonial history, identity crises, and the role of women writers in modern Ireland. This menu of issues amounted to an agenda and it became crystal-clear that *poetry* had very little to do with it except to serve as a springboard for someone else's flight of fancy. Their peers and history influenced Irish poets. OK. Game, set and match. As for Europe ...?

When I muttered something about coming from a Protestant background in Belfast and living in the west of Ireland, a professional smile glazed over what remained of our allotted time. Critical comment on that background – indeed, on any sense of alternative influences, arguments or literary ideals – went out the window.

Three random experiences. But behind them there are other conversations and impressions, which illustrate the kind of busy and processed responses poets in Ireland must resist in their work if they are to remain truly themselves as artists. There is, and probably always has been, a shifting agenda of themes and issues which 'Irish' literature is thought to address. But such crude generalisations are nevertheless influential both in a popular sense and in strict terms of criticism (i.e. what gets written about) because they underpin certain kinds of public space and esteem (i.e. recognition) in which the individual poet lives and writes. For the story goes that Ireland is coming down with poets. Certainly, it is much easier to have a poem or collection of poetry published in Ireland today than it was, say, twenty years ago. This is a good thing but what it really means in artistic and critical terms is another matter. All too easily, the books go unheeded in the literary pages of the newspapers and the few literary journals cannot hope to keep pace. Giving readings seems to be more important than having people read the poems. An undiscriminating media can all too often obliterate the work of art in a haze of well-meaning publicity surrounding this writer or that and their ability to make themselves and/or their writing 'accessible', 'controversial' and so forth. Where is the artistic daring, one asks, as the poem evaporates? Literary standards are equated with elitism or derided as academic when really it is 'period styles' that should be criticised – outdated or hackneyed themes; stale language; flat rhetoric; predictable feelings. Could there be, for instance, an equivalent version of Al Alvarez's *New Poetry*, the publication of which in the mid-1960s (with the brilliant Jackson Pollock *Convergence* as cover design) challenged so many imaginations and critical sensibilities, both old and new? Or of Donald Hall's updated version of Michael Roberts' *Faber Book of Modern Verse* whose presence on 'A' level courses throughout Britain and Northern Ireland during the late 1960s enlightened an entire generation of poets and readers in a handful of years, along with the marvellous BBC Radio school programmes on poetry, accompanied by their extraordinary texts?

The late 1970s and the 1980s really mark an epoch in which poets and poetry became sexy, an acceptable career move with its own structure of blandishments, self-promotion and sales-pitch at a time, ironically, of economic recession and political meanness.

But to go back to that term 'academic'. As someone who flits between two worlds – of trying to live as a writer and to help keep a roof over my family's heads through teaching – the extent to which the life of the intelligence is belittled in Ireland, often in a misconstrued support of the imagination, never fails to surprise me. Indeed, ignorance of the poetic traditions of writing is sometimes applauded as a *guarantee* of artistic integrity. This perverse and deeply damaging notion is related to the persistent, bathetic belief in the poetic 'personality' as a hero.

The problem is the basic uncertainty about the *value* of contemporary literary work, whereas the public role and social occasion of its expression are more eagerly integrated into the Irish literary culture. This avoids the awkward, time-consuming business of assessing, considering and vindicating artistic worth in favour of anecdotes over a jar.

As in our politics, personality is inflated with meaning and thence to the ghastly patronage of 'the character'. It is amazing, too, how many writers, including younger ones, seem to connive with this recognition. The main thrust of our generalisations about art, writing and the imagination (all such vague, abstract words, in comparison with the homely 'saying' of a poem) reflect this unease. For, in some deep-seated fashion, poets in Ireland must not take their work seriously. This is where the myth of the 'Irish poet' intercedes, bolstered very often by archaic ideas and misconceptions about the country as a whole. Irish writers are not, generally speaking, badly done by: their work is published relatively easily; there are various venues, festivals, art centres, magazines, television and radio programmes interested in promoting and conferring popular recognition on people as poets. The Arts Councils, north and south, on unjustly limited state budgets, do provide bursaries and other monies. Aosdána pays people to concentrate on their writing. UK and North American reading circuits, publishers, universities and so on are receptive to Irish poets. In other words, as poets, we do not actually suffer directly from repression, political violence, the loss of our language. ...

Yet, for all that, there *is* the sense of claustrophobia, of a kind of repression embedded in the culture and internalised by those writers conscious of their 'privileged' position within Irish society and troubled by both sets of circumstances. Familiarity may well breed a contempt of sorts when there is not sufficient *critical* respect given to the art of poetry. And there is, too, the business of just how independent writers in Ireland can be, given the close ties between the writing establishment, the state and the commercial world.

Who is looking at the effects and influences of this liaison upon standards in the arts? Does it lead to conformity or artistic compromise with a view to what gets bought, read or produced? Who are the people in Ireland entrusted with promoting standards in the literary and visual arts? What do we know of them; what are their qualifications in fulfiling such creative, editorial or judgmental roles?

Great hatred, little room? Not quite – more like anxiety, that verges on neurosis, surrounding the social and political orthodoxies, the conformism of a culture that is still morally and artistically unsure of itself. It is a culture, moreover, which is contradictorily ambivalent about its need for recognition from other cultures, particularly British and American, and peculiarly conscious of having to live up to their expectations of what it is, along with the sort of things we are meant to write about it.

II

In his excellent introduction to *Yeats* (1971) in the Fontana Modern Masters series, Denis Donoghue described Yeats' attitude to society in the following terms:

> his mind turns unwillingly to detail, unless the detail is a nuance of feeling. He admired notable people, but his respect for ordinary people as constituting a particular society and living a certain life at a certain time was extremely weak; when he looked beyond the chosen few he saw a fictive race rather than a finite society.

I am not sure that this is absolutely true since Yeats used the chosen few friends and companions as bridges into the wider world, a public world, and he operated there with enthusiasm and dedication; but the gesture Donoghue is describing seems representative in another way. For in our 'post-Yeatsian' Ireland we still think of 'the Irish' as a fictive race while 'a finite society' is quite clearly not a priority, and this holds true whether we are talking about the north or the south of Ireland. Society and civic space have evaporated into thin air, along with the assumed rights and responsibilities of our being, quite simply, citizens. This evasion, for such it is, has all kinds of implications for literature and literary criticism. It means, for instance, that the role of the writer in Irish society is intimately bound up with compensating rather than with questioning. In place of a social world, in which each citizen performs certain basic obligations and receives, in return, certain freedoms, our literary culture (in the main) shoulders this responsibility to become a chronicle of failure.

Failed obligations, inadequate freedoms – with the net result that Irish novels, poems, plays and criticism often deal with what is not the case rather than with what is. The writer's inheritance is to negotiate with the supposed ideal world, and the fall from such grace; the finite society exists elsewhere, like poor old England.

The reasons for this slippage are much too complicated to go into here but one cannot help noticing the extent to which Irish literature, and the critical reception it receives, is haunted by a greater past while the present is treated with disdain. Ireland *now* has to be bad news (or dressed up as a yuppie paradise!); the future or the past is infinitely better.

The political draft of this influence is plain to everyone. We do not have to look at the exact human effects of this or that political act because, basically, politics does not really happen in Ireland. What we have are messianic strategies, earthed in historical overviews and sacred landscapes or the job lottery of international 'diplomacy'. Talk to anyone under the age of forty, and hear for yourself the chief reason for the exodus from the country; read the poetry and prose that is produced week after week for publication in the few magazines and newspapers that bother to offer a decent platform for Irish writers at home. The message is quite emphatic: in spite of all the grand talk, 'Ireland' is breaking down. What will take its place is, of course, the big question.

Strangely, Denis Donoghue does not really give this much thought. On the very first page of *We Irish: Essays on Irish Literature and Society* (1986), he introduces the selection of essays and reviews with an unusual reservation:

> There seemed little merit in bringing forward an essay on Long Kesh and the Hunger-Strikes, which appeared in *The New York Review of Books* in October 1981; the issues raised by that event were immediate and intense, but it would be tendentious to bring them up again.

Just because something appears at one time 'immediate and intense' does not debar it from lasting significance. But the Hunger Strikes as 'tendentious'? Hardly. The Hunger Strikes represent the resurgence of militant republicanism as a populist force in Northern Irish politics. The ghastly point about the Hunger Strikes must surely be, as Seán O'Faoláin pointed out in his *London Review of Books* article at the same time, that they were (are?) part of an Irish belief in sacrifice, and that sacrifice is seen not as a denial of political possibility (as failure, in other words) but as its consummation. This denotes a remarkable relationship to the world. It is precisely around an issue like the Hunger Strikes that a whole series of cultural, spiritual and political assumptions surface and bring in their wake the dark secretive nuances of feeling that Yeats understood so much better than many a contemporary commentator. And after him, too, a poet such as Padraic Fiacc has constantly turned to that desperate, tragic strain in Irish experience. Yet Fiacc is not mentioned in Donoghue's 'The Literature of Trouble' as a poet, only as editor of the anthology *The Wearing of the Black* (1974).

When he is on firmer ground, such as 'The European Joyce' or the fine *Sewanee Review* piece, 'Together', Donoghue's intellectual arguments are precise and invigorating. It is disarming, though, in this battery of cross-reference and perceptive readings, to come upon another tilt in the direction of Stephen Dedalus' scene with the Dean of Studies and Seamus Heaney's refashioning of this 'acquired speech' for his own purposes in 'Station Island'. Donoghue is less than convinced, it has to be said, but one would have preferred a clearer critical conclusion to the title essay, 'We Irish', than the somewhat bemused (and bored?) remark: 'It is probably wise for some poets to brood as little as possible upon their being Irish and to let the constituents of their poetry settle down without fuss.' A touch disingenuous, or blankly ironic, given the title 'We Irish'?

Where Donoghue brings a slight sense of elevated dismay to his topics, Edna Longley comes out fighting in *From Cathleen to Anorexia* (1990), knowing the ropes (and who made them) like the back of her hand. Edna Longley has precious few illusions left about 'a fictive race'. She hates the sight of such blather and is understandably impatient, to the point of intolerance, with any writer who disagrees. Longley is for the finitude of society and the transcendence of art.

What I find most convincing about her pamphlet is that there are no holds barred, although I wonder if the literary discrimination occasionally slips in the interests of establishing a canonical hit list, from Field Day *via* John Hume to the taking to task of Eavan Boland for *A Kind of Scar: The Woman Poet in a National Tradition* (1989). Without going into the ins and outs of the question, it strikes me that Boland *does* question the 'National Tradition' – Longley thinks otherwise – as much as the male-dominated literary culture. She sees nationalism, after all, as 'a necessary hallucination within Joyce's nightmare of history', but obviously her disengagement is not sufficient for Edna Longley's purposes: 'because she [Boland] does not blame Nationalism, her alliterative muse turns out to be the twin sister of Dark Rosaleen: "the truths of womanhood and the defeats of a nation: an improbable intersection?"' The question is Boland's but Longley's rejection of the tentative answer is unconditional:

'Boland's new muse ... looks remarkably like the Sean Bhean Bhocht ... By not questioning the nation, Boland recycles the literary clichés from which she desires to escape.'

But questioning the nation might not lead anywhere either, as far as literature goes. As Edna Longley points out elsewhere, Virgin-Ireland as Proud or Sorrowful Widow, Defiant Daughter or Long-Suffering Mother are the kinds of images many Irish and British activist writers were brought up on. But how has the poetry, prose or drama been interpreted if not as just one more vehicle for voicing dissent from, or a need for, the 'fictive race'? Could it not well be that imaginative inspiration and vitality lie somewhere else altogether?

That said, the metaphorical question remains, to quote from Richard Murphy's 'The Battle of Aughrim': 'To whom will the land belong/This time tomorrow night?' The issue of authority and a negotiated settlement of power can be sublimated into as many texts as there are political prisoners, but only an honest, responsible and just constitutional structure can resolve it. From then on, people will make (or not make) the necessary adjustments, as was done in the Free State during its turbulent birth, and in every other European country, not to forget the struggle for civil rights in the United States, bloody debacle as that was.

In an instructive sense, we can see this prefigured in the poetry of Richard Murphy. In his *New Selected Poems* (1989) the development is from a poet preoccupied with the history of his family and its role in Irish life to the metaphorical home his poetry can build for himself, such as the sonnet sequence *The Price of Stone*. Ironically, Murphy has been shunted aside in much of 'the debate' so far. He does not feature, for instance, in Donoghue's 'Yeats, Ancestral Houses, and Anglo-Ireland' and one would have thought Edna Longley might have quoted his poem 'Amazement' as an apt illustration, alongside the Irish ballad of Paul Muldoon's 'Aisling'.

It may be that Murphy's knowledge of Irish life alludes paradoxically to a respect for ordinary people, for the particularity of their society, and that this manner, which amounts to the creation of an entire world in his poetry, has become unintelligible to contemporary ideological schemes. This would be a great pity because Murphy has bridged various kinds of cultural divide himself – between England and Ireland; the rich erotic world of Sri Lanka in *The Mirror Wall* (1989) and the imperial decay of Ceylon; the outcast in society and the possibility of freedom in the present day.

1990

III

In *The Dark Sun*, his book on D.H. Lawrence, Graham Hough remarked:

> The contrast between the provincial child-
> hood and the cosmopolitan later life has
> been overplayed. Childhood is always pro-
> vincial, and its horizon always restricted

> ... [a] rather hoity-toity concept of culture
> has been used to show that Lawrence
> had a hole-and-corner upbringing, and
> remained therefore an inspired barbarian,
> ignorant of the grand calm expanses of
> properly certified European civilisation.
> But the only people who ever inhabit
> this kind of civilisation are cultivated
> Americans, like Henry James or Mr. Eliot;
> Europeans live in Nottingham or Nancy,
> Paris or Piacenza, Frankfurt or Fenny
> Stratford, and the actual life of any of
> these places has always seemed a poor
> and disappointing affair to visitors from
> the platonic New England heights.

Hough's point is damning when we think of the
time and energy spent in Ireland riddling out Patrick
Kavanagh's now infamous distinction between
parochialism (a certain good) and provincialism (a
definite negative). Screeds have been filled, too, on the
topic of cosmopolitanism in Irish literature as against
the rootedness of Irish life. Indeed, the perceived
tension between the two has become a theme of much
contemporary writing in English: Heaney, Walcott,
Harrison, Murray ... inspired barbarians all.

As Hough says, we all come *from* somewhere;
where we go *to* is another question. Somehow, in
Ireland, there is a kind of sanctity about this original
relationship: an inherited piety, defying scrutiny, which
bobs around in an ether of accent, nudges and winks,

aspiration and ambition. We all *know* what is meant even as little change is ever made of home through imaginative and cultural interpretations.

Where one is from in Ireland, all that mire of anecdotage, which so often conceals an old-fashioned hunger for power, prestige and authority, defines 'the self' before one can literally open one's mouth. In recent times, the politics of place has taken over the place of politics in our lives. This is a shame. In a way, regionalism is some kind of answer.

When I think of regionalism, though, I think of the greatest provincial traditions in literature and the visual arts in France, or the example of a writer like Franz Kafka who engaged at such a deep imaginative level with his own religious and linguistic background in Prague. In Ireland, regionalism seems to mean something else entirely: *Dáil Connacht* in the late 1960s and '70s, or a group of fugitives seeking political time-out, a cultural breathing space in the 1980s. Or it assumes the double take of fidelity, using the culture one has come from as an imaginative and linguistic crutch before learning to walk, metaphorically speaking, in the big bad world. The vernacular as empire-breaker can so easily be turned inside out, especially by a culture, such as Britain's or Ireland's, which lacks powerful European-style provincial traditions in art and literature.

Honour, reserve, distance, understanding, anger, respect: these are all words that come to mind when one thinks about place. Region and regionalism are, instead, awkward substitutes designed to take out the heat but give little in return, other than the digital glow of an agenda, with its key words (identity and so forth) and expected social practices: dour northerners, slick Dubliners, dreamy westerners and the like.

For what it's worth, I come from no region called 'Northern Ireland', 'Ulster' or the 'Six Counties'. I come from Belfast, born and bred on the north side, schooled in the east; and in these particular districts, with known avenues and persistent views, attitudes and assumptions, my own speech was formed. Everything I write and say is conducted in and through that medium. What one does with such an inheritance calls upon chance, choice and the luck of the Muses. It is a recalcitrant, disturbed and unsettling past in the main and I find it hard to accept the vision many Irish writers have about 'home' as a substitute *literary* reality of consoling artifice. So art makes up for the impoverished present and past without which there would be no poem or play in the first place. One wonders where self-irony and a sense of proportion have gone when a comparison is made between contemporary Irish history and continental Europe of the post-1914 era.

Seamus Heaney, writing about Kavanagh and MacNeice in *The Government of the Tongue*, remarks that Kavanagh's achievement, whether he 'wanted it or not', 'was inevitably co-opted, north and south, into the general current of feeling which flowed from and sustained ideas of national identity, cultural otherness from Britain and the dream of a literature with a manner and a matter resistant to the central Englishness of the dominant tradition'.

When, however, Edna Longley calls the North 'a cultural corridor', regionalism is being brought into play. For Heaney's 'national identity, cultural otherness' read 'a zone where Ireland and Britain permeate one another'. The suggestion of fluidity here (*permeate*) is appealing, but the notion of boundaries (*corridor*) poses more problems that it can hope to solve. After all, corridors must lead somewhere and what might work in a poem (the translation of influences) is totally different to politics and the struggle for power.

It could well be that my own upbringing, in eluding strong cultural definition, paradoxically took too much for granted; that what looked like ease was really anxiety. So the thought that has crossed so many minds throughout these islands remains about *what* one actually belongs to – a state, a nation, a place, an idea, an illusion, or just images. Understanding where one has come from evokes a physical place but also a temporal order; the business of history, and how often the call is made for 'us' to master it.

In her excellent collection of essays, *Men in Dark Times* (1968), Hannah Arendt, who knew about exile and oppression, wrote:

> Insofar as any 'mastering' of the past is possible it consists in relating what has happened; but such narration, too, which shapes history, solves no problems and assuages no suffering; it does not master anything once and for all. Rather, as long as the meaning of the events remains alive

... 'mastering the past' can take the form of ever-recurrent narration. The poet in a very general sense and the historian in a very special sense have the task of setting this process of narration in motion and of involving us in it.

It does not matter what word you give this process so long as it happens. Where the poet fits in is, more than likely, to make poems that speak for themselves – the principal loyalty which has everything to do with a private sense of a place and its peoples.

1992

CHAPTER FIVE

OUR HIGH DESTINY

The first time I read Thomas MacDonagh's posthumous collection of lectures and essays, *Literature in Ireland: Studies Irish and Anglo-Irish*, I was a student at the University of Ulster at Coleraine. It was the early 1970s. At that time Northern Ireland was in the grip of 'the Troubles', although very few in those days had any idea that the recurrence of the political conflict in the North would last for twenty-five years. There was an intense need during the early 1970s for those of us who were politically grappling with what was happening to sort out what possible role writing could play in all the mayhem.

Writing poems had somehow to be called to account in an atmosphere of daily bombings and assassinations which were themselves becoming commonplace. It was a mistake, perhaps, to think that anything we could write would have an impact upon what was happening in the streets and townlands of the North but the desire was nonetheless there to find some kind of redress.

In the main, young writers I knew were looking abroad for answers: to the Russian poets like Mandelstam, Akhmatova; eastern European writers such as the Polish poet Zbigniew Herbert, Vasko Popa from former Yugoslavia, and the German Hans Magnus Enzensberger. We watched films like Wajda's *Ashes and Diamonds*, *Rome Open City* by Rossellini and Bergman's *The Shame*. Foreign shores are always greener.

Through lectures on literature in English, be they on Marlowe or Conrad, Coleridge or Larkin, it took some time before the cultural and intellectual ferment of what was happening all around us found a historical focus in Irish writing. The centrality of history in Irish writing, in both languages, and the kind of example of writers and intellectuals earlier in the century, is now a critical truism taken for granted by the generation that emerged from the shadows of the Troubles, north and south, in the 1980s and '90s. During the same period, Irish writing has been read worldwide as a laboratory within which the interpenetration of history, cultural nationalism and post-colonialism can be studied. Meanwhile, this history of political conflict and cultural attrition has become a theme park many inside Ireland would prefer to pass by. The murky old past is best left that way – in the past.

To discover in Thomas MacDonagh's *Literature in Ireland* a comprehensive, committed voice, calmly stating his position on the relationship between literature and history, was a revelation. The historical contexts of MacDonagh's own short life add poignancy to the writing such as one feels in regard to, say, the death of Wilfred Owen. Indeed, MacDonagh was well aware of what was taking place beyond his own political and imaginative life, as he remarks in the concluding paragraph of his own Preface in the book:

> It is well to let it be known that some of the studies [in *Literature in Ireland*] were written before the summer of 1914. The present European wars have altered our outlook on many things, but as they have not altered the truth or the probability of what I have written here, I have not altered my words. As will be seen, I anticipated turbulence and change in the arts. These wars and their sequel may turn literature definitely into ways towards which I looked, confirming the promise of our high destiny here.

Dated January 1916, only a matter of months before the Easter Rising for which MacDonagh, as a key figure and signatory, was condemned to death by British court-martial and executed by firing squad on 3 May 1916, the prophesy hangs upon those last few words with terrible irony: 'the promise of our high destiny here'. The terms of such utopian desire were sorely tested in the following decade and more: was the 'promise' of Irish cultural nationalism fulfilled? What 'high destiny' could attend a small island, exhausted economically and emotionally by years of constant expectation and ambition, a war of independence and civil war, and the eventual partitioning of the country into two self-insulated states? How would MacDonagh have responded, as a radical intellectual, to the enactment of the restrictive censorship laws of the new Free State?

Questions proliferate because of the sense of premature ending which surrounds the lives of the executed leaders of the 1916 Rising. If the Rising was, in Declan Kiberd's words, 'a brave clean fight against an empire', what are we to do with its perverse legacy in the North where the majority of the citizens did not fight against 'the empire' but *for* it? And to invest so much of their cultural and moral self-consciousness in that fact. What went so seriously wrong with the abundant idealism as there unquestionably was in 1916 (and later) that it should end in the grotesque parody of an imagined community, in the North, torn apart by self-inflicted and seemingly self-perpetuating violence? Was there something congenitally suspect in a nationalism that could not embrace the differences within the putative nation and was even to make a virtue out of refusing to imagine the problems it was storing up in the North? Must we still bear allegiance to that official wish-fulfilment simply for the sake of 'history'?

The answer is 'no' but, that said, there is in contemporary Ireland a reluctance to establish a clear idea of what the leaders of the Rising actually stood for; the cultural differences between them, and the (predominantly) secular and pluralist 'agenda' they pursued. What was their complex fate has been simplified into a marvellous self-sacrificing patriotic instinct carried through a fatal gene of bloodlust. Only with the dubious benefit of hindsight are definitive lines of direct connection forged between their vision and the version of it which church and state connived at and ultimately achieved.

These ideological and intellectual conflicts often appear claustrophobically obsessive and introverted in comparison with the airy, naïve, enthusiastic and fascinating study *Literature in Ireland*. MacDonagh's book radiates a serious but deft lyrical approach to poetry, as he cites *Poetry*, the Chicago journal, the Futurists, and other contemporary *vers libre* sources, to win the arch-modernist Ezra Pound's approval. Put at its simplest, MacDonagh sought to identify the linguistic and quasi-cultural factors (what he calls 'the Irish Mode') that will both establish and vindicate the separate nature of Irish literature. The idea for such a distinct identity had been hotly debated throughout the previous decade and more by all kinds of writers, intellectuals, political figures and activists. That there could be an Irish literature ('a separate thing', as MacDonagh states) was as potent an issue as the legitimacy and validation of an Irish state.

Throughout *Literature in Ireland*, MacDonagh argues his case with insight and due regard for the notion of other literatures in English. Walt Whitman has a major status in MacDonagh's intellectual and artistic universe. And *Literature in Ireland* anticipates many of the key issues with which critics and scholars have been involved throughout the twentieth century:

the influence of the Irish language and folk tradition upon Irish writing in English; the notion of literature being 'national' in the first place; the issue of race.

MacDonagh has important (and contentious) things to say about these and other issues. The rhetoric (in the strict sense) shifts register uncomfortably, and the range of literary reference is stretched beyond belief, but the key to this work is incontrovertible – MacDonagh's formulation of 'a movement that is important to English literature because it is in part a revolt from it'. Flowing from this premise, MacDonagh's task – 'to examine the one aspect of literature in Ireland that can be examined and treated in terms of criticism' – remains valid to this day. In searching out some of the co-ordinates of 'a new literature, the first expression of the life and ways of thought of a new people, hitherto without literary expression, differing from English literature of all periods, not with the difference of age but with the difference of race and nationality', MacDonagh anticipated much of the current discussion about the relationship between poetry, cultural politics and post-colonialism: or, in a word, difference.

Literature in Ireland, by a quirk of literary fate, became itself a part of the cultural assumptions underlying the post-independent Irish state and dutifully disappeared from critical view. Its unavailability as a critical key to the internal history of criticism in Ireland tells its own story. The language of the stereotypes, which MacDonagh often calls upon, certainly needs astringent deconstruction:

In spite of the self-consciousness of the age, in spite of the world influences felt here, in spite of all our criticism, the Irish poets and writers (those that are truly Anglo-Irish) are beginning it all over again in the alien tongue that they know now as a mother tongue. They delight not in the ink-horn terms of the English literary succession but in the rich living language of a people little affected by book-lore, a people standing but a little way on the English side of the crossways, remembering something of the syntax or the metaphor of Gaelic, much of the rhythm, inventing mostly for itself its metaphor from the things of its life, things known at first hand.

In terms of literary history, such a passage neatly summarises the main assumptions that became standard in the critical reception for, and expectation of, Irish writing at home and further afield.

Literature in Ireland is a classic expression of the case for the separateness and integrity of Irish national literary and cultural traditions. Whether or not we agree with MacDonagh, his collection of studies has a historical significance in the development of what became known worldwide as 'Irish literature'.

MacDonagh strikes me as the most reluctant of heroes. The much-quoted story of his last class at University College Dublin, on Jane Austen, before joining up with the insurgents, or the unattributed anecdote, retold by Terry Eagleton, to the effect that 'MacDonagh was one of the first men to be seen wheeling a pram in the streets of Dublin' suggest an individualist rather than a misguided fantasist, as he has often been depicted. Now is the time when Thomas MacDonagh can be seen for what he actually was, along with all the other men and women who believed, as he did, in Irish independence. For there is little point in blaming the long dead for present woe or merely revering them as our greater selves. As the Italian poet and film-maker Pier Paolo Pasolini remarked in *The Lutheran Letters*:

> It would be too easy, and, in a historical and political sense, immoral, if the sons were excused – excused in what is ugly, repellent, inhuman in them – by the fact that the fathers erred. The negative paternal legacy may half-explain them but for the other half they are themselves responsible.

It seems that much of what has been written and spoken about the last thirty years in Ireland boils down to a shift in recognition that the sons *are* as much responsible as their fathers. In fact, 'the negative paternal legacy' of Irish history has become a bit of a dead end, no longer answering the moral and political call of today. Somehow or other, the sons and daughters – of Ulster, of Ireland – have to catch themselves on, discard the myths that intrude between themselves and the reality of the country they live in. In Ireland, the chief enemy of positive change has always been piety: the need to sanctify and ritualise ourselves by way of compensation for what may well be the impoverished reality of our political culture. When *getting by* is no longer possible, the inevitable reaction is *blowing up*. It was the pig-headedness and arrogance of one political party (the Unionist), aided and abetted by the total disinterest and bloody-mindedness of another state (Britain) that forced a third sleeping partner (the Republic) into a kind of hyperbolic life, by which time it was too late.

Violence had taken root; lifestyles were formed almost exclusively around it – sacrifices, bitterness, despair, revenge. We were not so much back somehow in a place where this had all happened before (1913, 1916, the War of Independence, the Civil War, the 1950s' IRA campaign) but at each other's throats. Us. This part of Belfast against that part. Anonymous gruesome murders. A Jekyll and Hyde world of politics by day, assassinations by night. Ritual condemnations followed hard-necked tactical indifference. And it was naturally the 'ordinary people' who suffered. 'We told you so', and whoever 'we' were determined what was being told or sold. While time had moved on, history had not.

The North looks like becoming a place divided between recreational centres and theme parks on the one hand, and fictionalised epicentres on the other called 'West Belfast' or 'East Belfast', 'Bandit Country', where the struggle goes on. To get street-signs into Irish, to maintain the British way of life; to find an 'Irish', 'British' or 'Ulster Scots' identity is to be at home. Searching for identity is a complicated and difficult task. It takes insight, critical reflection, time, luck, laughter and, beyond all else, a realisation that the important things are never that obvious. Which is precisely why literature, painting, dance and music have become so central to an understanding of the present. Compared to continental Europe, however, our troubles are on a relatively small scale. But we do have one thing in common. In his 'Letter to Dr Gustav Husak', the Czech playwright and one-time President, Václav Havel, places before us that which we share when he writes of 'cultural self-knowledge':

> What mounds of mystification, slowly forming in the general cultural consciousness, will need to be chipped away? How far back will one need to go? Who can tell which people will still find the strength to light new fires of truth, when, how and from what resources, once there has been such thorough wastage not only of the fuel, but of the very feeling that it can be done?

I am not thinking here of cultural self-consciousness or revisionism. One leads to shocking and delusive transparency, while the other can atrophy any public will to act by destroying the ability (and possibility) of people *sharing* certain beliefs, hopes and feelings.

What Havel and the Czechs can teach us is twofold: to reach for scepticism when utopianism raises its (bloody) head while simultaneously acknowledging that:

> Visions of a better world and dreams about it are surely a fundamental aspect of authentic humanity; without them and without that transcendence of the given which they represent, human life loses all meaning, dignity, its very humanness … when an idea ceases to express the transcendent dimension of being human and degenerates into a substitute for it, the moment when the artefact, the project for a better world, ceases to be an expression of man's responsible identity and begins, on the contrary, to expropriate his responsibility and identity, when the abstraction ceases to belong to him and he instead begins to belong to it …

At that point life is lost to liturgy. The imagination – a viable, quiet, unexpected force in forging and disturbing the connections between the past, present and future – becomes mere propaganda; marketing fodder. Literature is the real time bomb; politics the space in which our necessary practical negotiations for a better life take place. Unfortunately, politics in Ireland, north and south, have been stunted and contaminated by violence. Democracy has suffered as a result and people's understanding of what democracy actually means requires recharging if the deadly mistakes of the past are not to be repeated. So it often falls to writers to act like bridges between the world of the imagination and the needed world of political change, without realising that one does not lead necessarily to the other. The writer's relationship with politics should always be critical, not a mouthpiece. Perhaps, though, we have something further in common with the Czechs. Like them, we have an ability 'of rising above oneself and making light of oneself". It is this 'dimension of distance' that needs substantial, persistent and enlightened support if we are ever going to realise that 'to understand each other does not mean to become like each other, only to understand each other's identity'.

1992–6

CHAPTER SIX

THE SOUND OF
THE SHUTTLE

The city we inhabit is a dream
And visions all her streets and all her
    towers.
                    Richard Rowley, 'City Dawn'

When John Keats went on a walking tour of Ireland
in 1818, his impression of Belfast, like his sense of 'the
rags, dirt and misery of the poor common Irish', was
far from dreamlike:

> We heard on passing into Belfast through
> a most wretched suburb that most
> disgusting of all noises worse than the
> bagpipe, the laugh of a monkey, the chatter
> of women *solus*, the scream of a macaw –
> I mean the sound of the shuttle. What a
> tremendous difficulty is the improvement
> of the condition of such people.

Since that time, Belfast has been identified as an industrial centre unsympathetic to the romantic imaginative spirit that a poet such as John Keats personified. If the linen shuttle has disappeared, to be replaced by the commuter-belt aeroplane, the afterglow of Belfast's industrial past persists. Time and time again, in the literature of the past two centuries and more, if and when Belfast is mentioned, it is as a city engrossed in commerce and hardened by the graft of industrialism. A city, that is, condemned, or at least disdained, for its lack of imaginative offspring or feeling for things literary. In *The Oxford Literary Guide to the British Isles* (1977), Belfast's 'literary connections' are defined as being 'mainly with those writers who were born here, but there is a dearth of monuments or places of pilgrimage'. That there could be 'a dearth of monuments' in such a monumentalised city as Belfast seems incredible, but the authors, Dorothy Eagle and Hilary Carnell, are probably correct about the 'places of pilgrimage' simply because Belfast, until comparatively recently, has usually been considered indifferent to the creation of art and literature. I would like to comment on the possible reasons why this should be so.

Little has been written about Belfast that is not a political, economic, statistical or sociological study, and even the religious studies seem humdrum affairs. My feeling is that critics, literary and cultural, have stayed away from looking at Belfast simply because it seemed a dour, unimpressive cousin to the cosmopolitan flamboyance of Dublin and that, fraught as it may well be with bloody themes, the romance of Dublin's twentieth-century history shines marvellously in comparison with the monotonous sectarian siren of the half-baked and surly Northern capital. This was to change, of course, in the late '60s and '70s when Belfast shot to world prominence as a political flashpoint, but the old-style caricature lasted like an iron mould. It was, and to some extent still is, a cast fixed in the hegemony of Protestantism, and, even while no such cultural edifice exists, the influence of Protestantism in all its manifestations has determined the city's sense of itself.

Indeed, it is all very well for Geoffrey Bell, in his book *The Protestants of Ulster* (1978), to talk of 'the Protestant way of life' through quotations from *Loyalist News* or *Orange Cross* and declare: 'That is what the Protestant culture is all about: Protestant supremacy, Protestant ascendency', but he comes no closer to understanding 'the Protestant way of life' than any hostile nationalist. Instead, he merely sneers at it, ignoring the fact that the aspects he concentrates on (the songs, the football, the work) could, with qualifications, be applied to working-class communities throughout these islands. The ascendency (or supremacy) of Protestantism is the key to understanding what is all too obvious in cultural terms regarding Belfast: namely, its restricted and suspicious sense of 'culture' as a natural aspect of individual and social experience.

In *Culture and Anarchy in Ireland 1890–1939* (1979), F.S.L. Lyons tackles the issue in some depth.

He talks about this 'simple culture' as being 'for most of its adherents, a non-literary one which did not encourage either reading or the writing of imaginative literature'.

So, while there are various poetic works towards the end of the eighteenth century (like those of Bishop Percy of Dromore) and the rural folk poetry chronicled by John Hewitt, the nineteenth century of William Allingham leads silently, lamely, towards Louis MacNeice: 'Few novels, little poetry, hardly any drama, attract the eye until the beginning of the twentieth century. This was not due so much to lack of talent, as to lack of interest and, more particularly, to lack of patronage.'

I am not sure that if the shipbuilder magnet Sir Edward Harland had cast his mind and money around we would have had a poet's or playwright's statue adorning the phalanx of the City Hall in the place of, say, Lord Dufferin, but the idea is intriguing all the same. What seems more to the point is when Lyons connects, implicitly, this cultural 'void' with the 'Protestant myth'. Here we are on solid ground.

As Lyons narrates, Presbyterianism, particularly in the east Ulster countryside, paved the way, through English and Scottish craftsmen and weavers of the seventeenth century, towards an accumulation of capital which, in turn, was converted during the nineteenth century into entrepreneurial power and prestige, a status of domineering influence throughout the business, social and cultural life of Belfast. It was this class (counterparts to the later emergent Catholic middle class in Dublin which Yeats came to despise) that imposed its own order on the unruly instability of modern Belfast.

In other words, like all myths, the Protestant myth was a constructed one: exploited by some for amassing huge profits, while the majority of others (passively, sometimes militantly) supported it for their own protection and incremental advancement. Translated into an act of faith, this myth, as Lyons points out, 'appealed to religious primitivism, but it also provided colour, poetry and its own kind of magic for ordinary drab lives'. The problem has always been why this 'magic' is transformed into the nightmare of bigotry and sectarianism? Why those 'deep reserves of emotion which the normal conduct of their religion kept in strict restraint, but which, largely because of that restraint, could build up from time to time into explosions of violent feelings and actions'.

John Wilson Foster may have indirectly uncovered one of the reasons for this transformation from magic into violence when he remarked, in his *Forces and Themes in Ulster Fiction* (1974): 'If the stereotype is to be believed, Protestants exhibit a narrower emotional range and a greater, more careful and, on the whole, less imaginative stability, a stability that owes itself to their Protestant religion, the mythless recency of their Irishness, and their Scottish patrimony.'

There is an important frame of reference being formulated here which places the Protestant myth in a new and creative perspective. For if the stereotype is believed *as a paradigm*, without any loss of face but as an acknowledgement of historical facts, *how* these facts – of plantation, battle, massacre, victory – become assimilated and related to political analysis and opinion is secondary to the way they are translated into imaginative or cultural terms. They become, that is, sources of reference which *clarify* identity, rather than counters of belief which *threaten* identity, as so often happens. It is this latter effect which will, according to Foster, 'reinforce the Protestants' unflattering self-concept and make them strengthen the psychic walls that not only protect but also confine and inhibit. For the Ulster Protestant who is conscious of his heritage and is not merely a peripheral Englishman, this self-consciousness is creatively crippling.'

Or not as the case may be, since Foster and Lyons do not consider that the Protestant myth can become a source of imaginative *strength* as much as one of imaginative debility. Similarly, Belfast has more recently become a critical influence on the development of culture (primarily literary) in Ireland, rather than the Medusa it was conveniently taken to be. In the years ahead, my hope is that this 'Protestant Myth' will find itself less under the perplexed gaze of the shocked troops of British and Irish liberalism and be seen much more in the round, as a complex social organism.

Again, perhaps Lyons has anticipated this possible shift when he talks of 'the dualism of militant Protestantism', that residue of historical imperatives he describes elsewhere in his book, with its visible contrasts such as those found in the 12 July celebrations. Between the 'brilliant barbarity of the setting, its noise and glitter' and the 'sobriety of the serried ranks of grim, serious and utterly respectable marchers' one finds, in Lyons' terms, 'a formidable juxtaposition': the 'immobility and the dynamism of Protestant culture which mingles resolution and hysteria, siege and deliverance in a volatile dialectic'.

One need only consider Lyons' use of the word 'hysteria' to disclose the intimate range and depth of Protestant feeling. For as 'they' see it, Belfast is 'their' city, the birthright that has been terribly maltreated. Hence we find the recurrent dream of deliverance from this desperate situation. But deliverance means not only 'setting free'; it also means 'a giving up' or 'giving over', almost a 'surrendering'. It is against this reading that the other two psychologies come to bear: of siege and resolution, the steeling of an army and the maintenance of its absolute vigilance. These seemingly hectic gyrations of feeling can be likened to the cacophonous movement of Keats' shuttle, drowning out the personal voice of imaginative expression.

Unquestionably, after much pain and delusion, Protestants are coming to the realisation, induced by the disinterest of Britain, that they must reconsider their own past, not as a gesture of 'sell out' or 'compromise', but simply to know themselves better and also to know what the future may hold. In this angry, inarticulate and bloody process, Keats' elevated opening to the first version of 'The Fall of Hyperion', written around the same time as his experience of Ireland, has a telling ring to it:

> Fanatics have their dreams, wherewith
>   they weave
> A paradise for a sect; the savage, too,
> From forth the loftiest fashion of his
>   sleep
> Guesses at heaven; pity these have not
> Traced upon vellum or wild Indian leaf
> The shadows of melodious utterance,
> But bare of laurel they live, dream, and
>   die;
> For Poesy alone can tell her dreams, –
> With the fine spell of words alone can
>   save
> Imagination from the sable chain
> And dumb enchantment. Who alive can
>   say,
> 'Thou art no Poet – may'st not tell thy
>   dreams?'
> Since every man whose soul is not a clod
> Hath visions and would speak, if he had
>   loved,
> And been well nurtured in his mother
>   tongue.

Just how the 'Protestant' community 'hath visions and would speak' is difficult to imagine, given the depth of prejudice that has characterised its sense of a community being at odds with the rest of the country in which it lives. My own experience might be relevant here. Having spent many years uncritically accepting the caricatures of the Protestant North from which I come, I found that it was only after I had left Belfast that I started slowly to explore the feelings, beliefs, attitudes, experiences and history of the Protestants in that part of Ireland. It was a strange sensation of uncovering, under the layers of bigotry, delusion and uncertainty, the human relation of the Protestants to their own past. Even while I still stood (and stand today) politically outside and critical of that relationship, I realised that nothing would ever materially change unless people started from the human story rather than from the theoretical premise. What's more, the crux of the matter for someone who writes poems, was that I knew I could achieve a kind of imaginative coherence for myself only if I looked deeper at how my Protestant upbringing had influenced me. This meant exploring this background and examining its cultural and literary expression in the Ireland of today. My feeling is that poems should speak for themselves, and that poets should let their poetry do just that, so I will not be referring to my own. Instead, I want to take a look at what the term 'Protestant imagination' can possibly mean in a few literary examples. My choice is, it must be stressed, a personal one.

Even though both attended Trinity College, a world of difference separates Oscar Wilde from his peer Edward Carson. Though they went their own ways, fate or whatever it is that tumbles us in one direction instead of another, drew them together again. I refer to A.T.Q. Stewart's book, *Edward Carson* (1981):

> Carson had been crossing the Strand one day when he was almost knocked down by a fine carriage drawn by two horses. The carriage stopped and out stepped Carson's old college contemporary, Oscar Wilde. Wilde was at the very height of his fame as a playwright and a literary lion in London society, one whose witticisms were attentively gathered and repeated in drawing-rooms throughout the country. He had become plump and prosperous; his countenance bore all the marks of high living and self-indulgence, and he was flamboyantly attired, exhibiting a white carnation in his buttonhole. 'Hullo, Ned Carson. How are you?' he said affably, stretching out his hand, which Carson shook. 'Fancy you being a Tory and Arthur Balfour's right-hand man! You're coming along, Ned. Come and dine with me one day in Tite Street'. Carson had never liked Wilde, but he was touched by his friendliness. Had he accepted the invitation, Wilde's tragic history might have been different, for it was Carson's strict rule never to appear against anyone from whom he had accepted hospitality. The brief which Russell now offered him was

to defend the Marquess of Queensberry against a charge of criminal libel and the prosecution had been initiated by Wilde.

The exchanges between these two men – both Irish Protestants – reveal something that it is important to grasp and relate to that other image involving Carson. There is a critical turn in the cross-examination where Carson, defending the Marquess of Queensberry, begins doggedly to undermine Wilde's confidence and studied flippancy:

> The climax of this remarkable cross-examination was reached when Carson asked Wilde about a boy called Grainger, who was Lord Alfred Douglas's servant in Oxford. 'Did you kiss him?' Carson asked. For one fatal moment Wilde's quick wits deserted him. 'Oh dear, no,' he replied without thinking. 'He was a peculiarly plain boy. He was, unfortunately, extremely ugly. I pitied him for it.' Carson pounced like a tiger. Was that the reason Wilde had never kissed him? Suddenly Wilde was on the verge of breaking down. 'Oh, Mr. Carson, you are pertinently insolent'. But Carson continued his remorseless questions. 'You sting me [Wilde declares] and insult me and try to unnerve me and at times one says things flippantly when one ought to speak more seriously. I admit it.' At this Carson gathered together his papers and sat down.

Wilde is defeated. But it is only the beginning of the end for him. Within three years, he was dead. Meanwhile, Carson received many congratulations for his handling of the case and, though reserved in his moment of triumph, he obviously took pleasure in his success. As Stewart has it: 'The sun-god [Wilde] had fallen abruptly to earth, humbled by the plodding contemporary [Carson] he had tried to patronise.' Many years later, with Wilde disgraced, imprisoned and dead in a hotel room by the turn of the new century, Carson has been reborn as saviour of the Unionist cause in the tempest of the Irish nationalist independence movement. Seventy thousand Protestants, some of whom had actually physically drawn Carson's carriage in Belfast one September day in 1912 – and their pleading with him to stay – suggests a desperate need of a people who see themselves as being fatherless, leaderless and hero-less. In that situation, the unlikely figure of Carson becomes *their* Liberator. In 1895 he had proved his powers of advocacy in destroying the dandified Wilde. Now he is the reluctant host of Fortune.

Some may baulk at the very notion of hero worship but the fact of the matter is that to many thousands of Protestant Unionists, Carson represented a kind of freedom and an identity being confirmed. Or, to put this in slightly different terms, he was an imaginative focus, a dramatising of themselves through his portrayal as an uncompromising, rigid protector of 'Truth'. That this image should be established during a crucial period in the history of Ireland (the 1890s to 1910s) tells us something about the Protestant imagination in the country.

It was effectively from this time, just prior to the World War I, that the Protestants in the North became increasingly more isolated from the rest of the country, while those living in what is now the Republic had to choose on what political or cultural grounds they would define themselves: Irish, Anglo-Irish, English, British. Eventually, marooned within their own state-let, the Protestants of the North had no other source of imaginative stability than the unexplored, hasty formulation of a Carson, who was not only unsympathetic to the aesthetic decadence of a Wilde, but incapable of seeing beneath its glittering and witty surface. The possibility, then, of an alternative imaginative tradition being 'officially' sanctioned or even fostered in the North, as was the case in the Republic, was most unlikely. Whatever creative springs there were could be tapped only by the populist displays of mass demonstrations, pacts and sacred covenants, dogmatically separated from the historical developments of the rest of the country. Until, that is, the poet John Hewitt started to bind the wounds and seek (tentatively) an imaginative *détente* with his peers in the rest of Ireland from the late 1920s onwards.

But I do not want to list those occasions, either in this century or in earlier ones, when Protestants from the North and the Republic, made effective efforts to absorb and transform 'Irish culture' into their own image. I want, instead, to consider the phrase

'Protestant imagination' and ask if such a thing exists in the first place.

If we accept that, with a personality like Carson so influential in the formation of 'modern' Protestant unionist ideology (and with men like James Craig about to follow), it was unlikely that the state formed out of that ideology would foster an imaginative literary tradition – then we should consider the response elsewhere in Ireland and what better place than in Yeats' poems and those published in *Responsibilities* (1914).

This volume is a central one in Yeats because it marks a change of tone – the poems become starker and more realistic; they question the dreamy Celticism of his previous work and turn, often with bitterness, upon the nationalist leaders of a cause Yeats had long espoused (independence from Britain and the fostering of a national literature) but which he saw turning into narrow dogma. *Responsibilities* records his disillusionment.

'September 1913', a key poem in the collection, is unmistakable in its attitude of scorn, bred of disenchantment with a dream:

> Was it for this the wild geese spread
> The grey wing upon every tide;
> For this that all that blood was shed,
> For this Edward Fitzgerald died,
> And Robert Emmet and Wolfe Tone,
> All that delirium of the brave?
> Romantic Ireland's dead and gone,
> It's with O'Leary in the grave.

Romantic Ireland was 'dead and gone' in Yeats' mind and, in registering this, the poet, who had helped create 'Romantic Ireland', touches upon one of the common elements of the 'Protestant' imagination – its insistence on measuring Irish dream against Irish reality and a reluctance to embrace what is often seen as an impoverished reality. It took James Joyce to accept and celebrate that. The great dream of a united culture, of a people actively committed to literary ideals, broke up under the pressure of actual political manoeuvring and the material needs of an ascendant and deeply conservative middle class. Yeats records this disillusionment as an activist, as one who worked tirelessly in promoting cultural idealism. In stark contrast, Samuel Beckett started off, twenty years later in *More Pricks than Kicks* and *Murphy*, from that point of disillusionment, made fun of it and debunked the entire notion of an Irish literary culture united, one and all. Then he left the country, more or less, for good.

In Beckett, we find an avoidance of nationalism and any other 'ism' or generalisation such as Protestant, which he sees as limiting the deeper search for personal identity. His Dublin Protestant middle-class background, however, guaranteed an isolation which attendance at the Trinity College of the late 1920s only confirmed. This suggests a further characteristic of the Protestant imagination – of *having* to think about one's cultural position, of being literally 'self-conscious'. Beckett represents the perfect example of an artist who, because of his background, is from the outset forced to question his own identity. In a way, his work parallels the actual historic situation of Protestants in Ireland. For, surely, that painful process of finding out 'what we are' characterises the present state of Northern Protestants? Yet many are frightened of accepting that question and hide behind the sternest preacher; others are prepared to face the uncertainty of the time or else leave it all behind them and emigrate.

For the Protestant *lack* of a 'recognised' cultural home (there is, after all, no such thing as *British* literature) has created a sense of displacement which inspires the excessive proclaiming 'We are British'. The situation is, of course, much more complicated than I am making it out to be and for a comprehensive examination of this question of identity, David Millar's *Queen's Rebels: Ulster Loyalism in Historical Perspective* (1978) is excellent.

The further twist in this distorted and distorting process of identity is the way the Protestant community in the Northern Ireland is conventionally seen as an introverted, imaginatively dull and uncreative source for an artist or writer. One need think only of how often the place has been characterised as 'dour' and even the 'black' of the Black North seems to blank out all possibility of imaginative light.

To challenge this crippling stereotype would also be fundamentally to question foreign perceptions of Ireland and the Irish as wild and imaginative, tripping over themselves with frothy language. More importantly, it might make the Irish reconsider their own self-image in cultural and political terms.

The final writer to whom I will refer has led many readers and critics to make these very necessary reconsiderations. The Belfast-born poet Derek Mahon reveals in his work a sympathetic understanding of the Protestant community. It is as though, at long last, Oscar Wilde is turning the tables on Edward Carson. Mahon's poem 'Nostalgias' (originally called 'The Chair Squeaks') defines that sense of aloneness which seems to be fundamental to both the Protestant community and also the 'Protestant' writer:

> The chair squeaks in a high wind,
> Rain falls from its branches;
> The kettle yearns for the mountain,
> The soap for the sea.
> In a tiny stone church
> On a desolate headland
> A lost tribe is singing 'Abide With Me'.

'A lost tribe': if that is the Protestant community, then the poets whose roots are sunk deep in that community are probing where the real world is (and not the one so many want to believe is the real one – of a Glorious Empire and deliverance from hordes of marauding 'Fenians') and making it possible, imaginatively, for others to begin to see their horizons and different possibilities.

In many of Mahon's poems, a mirror is held up in which the Northern Protestant community can see itself. In the unflattering conclusion to 'Ecclesiastes', he comes closer to understanding the nature of that community than any poet I know:

> Your people await you, their heavy washing
>   flaps for you in the housing estates –
> a credulous people. God, you could do it, God
>   help you, stand on a corner stiff
> with rhetoric, promising nothing under the sun.

While in a poem like 'Going Home', originally 'The Return', dedicated to John Hewitt, an appropriate symbol is created of the tenacious spirit that so often cripples Northern Protestants instead of inspiring their confidence in the necessity and management of change:

> Rooted in stony ground,
> A last stubborn growth
> Battered by constant rain
> And twisted by the sea-wind
>
> With nothing to recommend it
> But its harsh tenacity …

Of course, reading a poem will never subdue a bigot or dissolve the political divisions inherited from sectarian attitudes. It might, however, open the door to look anew at history, the individual's place in it, the willing and frank acknowledgement of what has been done in their name and the possibility thereby of transforming this experience into a sustaining and creative one. The choice is clear: either this is achieved or the myths that Northern Protestants live by will petrify further into fear, hatred and the self-disgust that goes with the debilitation of what is seen to be their greatest strength – their historical will. Only then can a proper dialogue begin between the different traditions in the whole country.

Or as Joseph Campbell remarked in *The Masks of God*, 'the opening, that is to say, of one's own truth and depth to the depth and truth of another in such a way as to establish an authentic community of existence'.

1983

CHAPTER SEVEN

A KIND OF COUNTRY

By the late 1980s, cultural self-consciousness in Ireland was fast becoming a civil service, literary duty and academic obligation. What was once an accent, an idiom, a voice turns into community action, a manifesto, a speech, a categorical imperative. There is nothing inherently 'wrong' in all this, so long as it is not predicated upon social engineering. For cultural identity has itself become a term much used and abused. In Ireland, it is thrown around like a Frisbee; terms such as Irish, British; nationalist, unionist; Protestant, Catholic. But what does identity actually mean, or, more importantly, are people really so preoccupied with it in Ireland as compared with people in Britain, France or the United States? Certainly, with the firebreak of the ceasefires, the first real signs of political reality broke through years of noxious and suffocating insularity. But like most people in Ireland, I have been a spectator at the game, not even sure of the rules or the players.

Observing what is happening in and to one's country can be a strange and estranging sensation. It can be a bizarre experience listening to language being put through the mill. From my own experience, for instance, when a unionist politician talked about 'Eire' as a poor, backward country, run by priests, I had to pinch myself. Is this the same place where I have lived for the past twenty years? The loyalist notion that the Irish state was massing on the border, either physically, metaphysically, or constitutionally, to take over Ulster, that jewel in the crown, was simply defying reality. Whereas republican rhetoric about an Ireland 'Gaelic and Free', a proud and sorrowful nation weeping and/ or dancing at the crossroads, was in as sorry a state of delusion when compared with the reality and cultural priorities of the Republic, here and now. I suppose this compares with the dream world which many believe in concerning the 'Great' in Great Britain, the 'United' in United Kingdom, with the 'might' of mighty England at the epicentre.

Whatever about the incontrovertible right of spokespersons to entertain such views, the fact that people killed and died for versions thereof in Ireland and Britain is chillingly beyond belief. Like many others who consider themselves to be British, the Protestants of Northern Ireland, who have kept themselves insulated in the comforting nostalgia called 'The British Empire', needed to step into the actual world. For a start, they had to recognise what had happened to and in Britain during the years of the 'Troubles'.

When the Thatcherite era imploded, shattering along the way national institutions and civic assumptions and services, what was left was a demoralised, unemployable underclass, a confused educational system, a health system in crisis, a civic environment ravaged by privatisation, a political caste tarnished by financial corruption and enfeebled by the lack of any vision and a culture weak in the public confidence to debate within itself its own future. More so than at any previous time in the twentieth century, there is now a radical (visionary, if you like) challenge of reimagining all the constituent parts of England, Scotland, Wales and their ties with Ireland.

This does not mean abandoning the past and all those influences and experiences which hundreds of thousands, indeed millions, share at various different levels throughout the islands. Specifically, the cultural history of the Northern Protestants is a complex and challenging history, emblematic of much that is still repressed in the Ireland of today while embarrassing in its militant nostalgia to the intellectual and media elite of Britain. Sadly, all too often, their story, the Protestant story, is patronised or distorted by journalists and other writers who are frustrated by the seemingly time-locked nature of the Northern Protestant culture, as if it only paralleled (or parodied) the intellectual complacency and inertia of a caricatured version of the English establishment. Protestants who believe in the union, who see, in other words, London as their capital, and Manchester, Birmingham, Leeds, Edinburgh, Cardiff as like-minded and as 'British' as themselves, and all those who believe in democratic rights, should have absolutely nothing to lose, or fear, from speaking their mind on the arguments about why the union should remain. Far too often, however, all one hears from Belfast and London is rant about a mysterious cultural 'link', while outdated nationalist rhetoric obscures the acute, deep-seated economic and cultural realities that continue to bind together both islands, howsoever political history has driven them apart.

My own deepest wish, for what it is worth, is that along the way to peace and justice, genuine common traditions and experiences of Northerners are reclaimed from the nightmare of the past. It would be foolhardy to assume, however, that cultural reprogramming and therapy will do the trick; as if unionists who are Protestant are merely closet Irish who need to come out. Many already see themselves as Irish. And many others do not. Others see themselves as British and Irish. So what? Is there not a community known as Irish-American? 'Hybridity'– where are you now when we need you?

No matter what 'solution' is arrived at, it seems that they will more than likely remain outside it; against the current, as symbols of a deeper malaise confounding both countries. By their very existence, they threaten easy notions of cultural unity inside Ireland while reminding post-industrial Britain of its colonialist and imperialist past. Indeed, it is not stretching credibility too far to suggest that the Protestants sum up the problems that lie ahead for Britain if and when a written constitution and a radically revisioned state become a central and necessary part of the political agenda. The difficulties that the Northern Protestants are experiencing in the present, anticipate the internal wrangling and doubts the English will have to go through if they are to find new, enabling mythologies for a secular, multicultural republic embracing Scotland and Wales.

Saying the words 'a secular, multicultural republic' in the present climate of English debate makes the very idea seem, at the same time, far-fetched and urgent. No wonder then that the Protestant community, in rejecting a comparable possibility within an Irish republic, were caricatured as introverted, imaginatively dull and uncreative: terms by which the English are often similarly defined.

In whichever direction the Northern Protestant community turned, its self-image was distorted, like the mirrors in a kaleidoscope, into grotesque parody: loud-mouthed invective, 'anti' everything, untranscendent, glum. This short-circuit, of ignoring their positive and artistically rich inheritance, is historically a complicated and fascinating example of cultural amnesia and artistic distortion. It disempowered writers and artists within their own culture from the 1930s to comparatively recent times and led to a failure of educational will, critical blindness and institutional complacency going back generations. This in turn affected the entire Northern community's self-consciousness (or at least those who gave even a cursory look at such matters). The effects, however, were particularly disabling for the Protestant sense of culture, missing, as it did, an immediate access to the counterweight of Irish literary and cultural traditions while averting its gaze from the US and (when the time came) Europe. Out of such uncertainties and contradictions, the stereotypical clichés of 'Britishness' vis-à-vis 'Irishness' in the North were eventually fed back into the eruption of civil unrest.

The buried prejudices that grew out of the absurdly partitioned Irish state came to haunt the country with a vengeance, and we have been paying for these bloody mistakes of the 1920s ever since and on all sides of the Irish Sea. Some take arrogant satisfaction in this situation, the 'Ship the Prods Back' mentality; others see Northern Protestant intransigence as an example of those historical facts and cultural conditions that require imaginative exploration, not exploitation. The shout of hundreds of thousands of Northern Protestants, 'We are British', is loudest in an effort to convince themselves of the fact; it is a collective whistling in the dark – emotional, deep-seated and involuntary.

The icons, flags and emblems of the British state are revered all the more intensely and intimately at such times when their self-belief and concepts of right are scorned. There are parallels that can be pursued between the Northern Protestant situation today, and what might emerge in England in, say, twenty-five years when ordinary English men and women can no longer take for granted the stability and reliability of a given history and a cultural identity based unthinkingly upon the post-World War II past.

The British are living in an interregnum, but facing the wrong way around. Depressingly, many of the clichés surrounding the Northern Protestant culture are recycled in Britain as much as in the Republic of Ireland, and further afield in the US. I could cite numerous examples, both personal and professional, but one will suffice. In 1994 *The Guardian* (16 July) ran a feature article entitled 'An Irish Answer' which was billed as 'a look beyond the prevailing images of northern culture': 'To find artistic fulfilment [means] to look beyond confines of the protestant world. To remain in a world where "culture" is restricted to little more than flute-bands, Orange marches and the chanting of sectarian slogans at football matches.'

The ignorance of that 'little more' is staggering but not, alas, very surprising. Not one mention of the many writers, historians, scientists, musicians, medics, who have come from that 'protestant world'. Imagine if such terms were used to describe the Irish or West Indian community in England, what justifiable rage there would be against such gross caricatures. Yet it is what writers have consistently had to face in Ireland (irrespective of the community from which they come) when stereotypes and cultural imperatives eclipse scholarly and critical enquiry into actual artistic accomplishment and ambition.

The significance of this unease plays across the cultural and political life of Belfast, London and Dublin and it will intensify confusingly when the stakes of revision (in terms of cultural authority and prestige) mount higher in the years ahead. A fate the

Irish have experienced in full measure may await the British as 'Englishness' literally becomes a thing of the past. National myths, in other words, undergoing renovation and revision can turn into a spider's web, catching the individual artist's impulse to write with freedom out of his or her own self.

A poem of mine, 'The Aunt's Story', which opens the collection *Heart of Hearts* (1995), is about my being in London in 1963. I was both a stranger and a subject, conscious, like millions of others, of my difference, yet also feeling partly at home. It slowly dawned on me, as Neal Ascherson comments on a similar experience in his marvellous collection of essays, *Games with Shadows* (1988), that 'my sense of awe at the Providence which had mysteriously allotted me Britishness – that had gone'. 'The Aunt's Story' is about such a realisation, as loss and as liberation:

> That first time in London, a family
>   wedding.
> I had my new school uniform on
> and Great Uncle Bill stood in the perfect
>   garden
> of his home telling me to spell *character*.
> The cats sat blinking in a far-off corner
> and Eileen – 'she never lost the accent' –
> watched her sister's grandson perform.
> The sky was bright as could be.
>
> What walked in the shadow was The
>   War,

the long road back, the swish of evening
    gowns,
as the girls crept in late to the god-awful
    groan
of their father in his own bedroom;

the half-opened door, the give-away
    stairs.
Her face at the kitchen window has the
    look
of someone distracted by what never was.
'C-h-a-r ...'

A poem should stand by and for itself but 'The Aunt's Story' brings to mind a few personal references to what I've been thinking about in general here. When I had originally completed this poem, I thought it was simply about one particular experience, translated into a storyline, as 'the' past and present criss-cross and turn into fictional reality. Now I see the poem differently. 'The Aunt's Story' records how personal identity, grounded in language as one's vision of one's self ('character'), is not quite achieved by the young boy's hesitant deliberations ('C-h-a-r'). The grammar of consciousness is predicated upon inherited and unquestioned ways of seeing and 'being' – The War, the patriarchal male presences, authority.

All these hints and allusions converge into one simple story of hearing how one says what one says, what one 'sounds like', the preserved accents of exile, the fictionalised community of the past. When consciousness is reified and made, however benignly, into a figure of amusement, the psychological impact mirrors the ever-changing balance of cultural and political power. Poetry registers the flux and subtext at the unpredictable and volatile level of language. Such tension is what makes poetry *poetry*. In the early sixties, the setting for 'The Aunt's Story', this kind of self-consciousness was free-floating and non-programmatic. By the nineties, when the poem was rewritten, every fibre of cultural and artistic awareness is drenched in demotic sensitivity to such an extent that contemporary literature (and the arts 'in general') are now almost exclusively interpreted (in the academy and in the media) in terms of certain pre-emptive categories of post-colonialism, ethnicities, gender, sexuality and race. All too often these categories become self-fulfilling predictions, a kind of intellectual wiring for 'sound bites'.

In *Literary Englands* (1993), David Gervais, discussing Philip Larkin, John Betjeman and the aftermath of 'England', remarks that 'far from being the option of the sentimentalist, nostalgia has become a living part of our culture, something we may sometimes feel stuck with but not something we can simply wash our hands of. It is in this sense that I believe it is possible to think of England as "the aftermath of England"'. Somewhat earlier, Gervais draws attention to several books that 'seek to colonise the past in the interests of their own particular version of England': 'What they look back to may vary; what they have in common is the act of looking back. Nostalgia is itself a kind of country, a focus of shared feelings through which we can acknowledge our nationality without relapsing into mere nationalism.'

The battle for cultural and political hegemony – who validates and legitimises the 'authentic' version of the past, for which reasons and with what effect on artistic values and critical recognition – should not obscure the dynamic, wayward and unforeseeable power of the imagination to dramatise the irretrievably human consequences and desires of our simply being here, randomly in one place, rather than in another.

1994

CHAPTER EIGHT

WHAT'S THE STORY?

For many unquestioning years from the mid-1970s, I taught English Literature at universities in Ireland – Shakespeare, Milton, Keats, the Victorians, the English novel, and so on. Of more recent years, since the mid-1980s, I have been teaching Irish writing – Yeats' poetry, *Dubliners* by Joyce, Beckett's plays, Elizabeth Bowen's 'Irish' novels, amongst it all. This period of time up to the present, let's say twenty-five years or thereabouts, has seen an extraordinary change in the way that literature is taught, tradition conceived, and the canon established. English literature is, in a sense, no more.

The decline and fall of the British Empire, of which we never tire of hearing and reading about, with its last final heroic gesture of sacrifice during World War II, has led (some would say inevitably) to the unravelling of English literature. The assumption, strength and myth underpinning English literature was that it was one continuous, monolithic present and presence in the cultural life and artistic community of those who read, teach or write books in the English language, or translate that literature into other languages and cultures. This belief has been shattered.

Irish writers have played a profound and continuing part in this subversive, subterranean and exhilarating process of altering and playing with various states of literary (and therefore linguistic) self-consciousness. But I agree with Declan Kiberd when he warns against oversimplifying this process:

> To see writing from Scotland, Ireland, or Wales as by definition anti-canonical seems to me to simplify a complex situation to the point of uselessness. For one thing the very canon of Eng. Lit. is to some extent a creation of outsiders such as Eliot; for another, many Irish writers, like their Scots counterparts, were remarkably keen to present themselves and their work in canonical terms.

One has only to go back 100 years to the release from an English gaol of the Irish playwright and critic Oscar Wilde, to realise just how central Irish writers have been in the appropriation of English as a form of liberation struggle against a dominant, conceited and morally impecunious imperial ruling class, such as the Victorian British bourgeoisie. Wilde paid for his victories as artist by being punished for his sexuality – a gay father of two, in love with his own ability to expose the hypocrisies and delusion of traditional English 'Society' and the artificiality of its language.

In this breaking down or devolution of 'English Literature', as Robert Crawford has called it, many different discourses have converged. It is a multi-faceted process that has taken place throughout the literary and academic world, leading to the creation of self-governing, or part-seeming, self-governing bodies called 'Irish Studies', 'Scottish Studies ('British Studies' didn't seem to take off), post-colonialism, gender studies, ethnicity, hybridity, Third World Studies. These potent terms of reference assume a fascinating and rigorous arsenal of analytic tools and political procedures, which have opened up the whole meaning of literary study and critical debate. They have forced a fundamental re-evaluation of the function of English literature, not exclusively in terms of the academy, but in the wider world of cultural production, via the media and the literary and artistic priorities of the publishing world, the theatre and so on. The impact on writing of this rethinking is still uncertain and unpredictable. Take 'Irish writing' as an obvious example.

As we keep reminding ourselves, Ireland is currently undergoing significant sea changes. Some of these are difficult to fathom; others are very much on the surface. These changes are obviously related to the various political manoeuvrings that have taken place during the past ten or so years to bring to an end the war over the political status of Northern Ireland. 'The North' is the symbolic focus that separates the local structures of the past from the not-yet-imagined structures of the future. And one can read this condition allegorically alongside the events of 'eastern' Europe, or, more realistically, as the bloody version of and precedent to the redefinition of the British Union. The North functions as a shifting parallel, or roving thematic, between Ireland and Britain, destablising stereotypical notions of 'Irishness'. That history is a well told story by now.

Religious and cultural differences that underpin Northern Irish society, and which once played an equally important and defining influence in southern Irish society, these differences of Protestant and Catholic, are systemic and institutionalised. The provincial Northern society of one and a half million people effectively accepted the fact that its children and young adults would live their lives educationally in separate, if parallel, schools. Depending upon one's religious background, schooling conformed to, and in its turn, confirmed, the political and cultural affiliations of one's own community.

The individual, born into division, could find the common bonds of civic society only by chance or through deliberate desire; an often perilous journey. From childhood, for instance, Protestants were taught, in the main, British history and read mostly English literature; Catholics were schooled in Irish history, learnt Irish as a language, while also learning about English literature. Schooled in this way, independent of one another, both traditions were defined by distinctive religious, political and cultural codes and priorities which have determined the actual nature of Irish civic society until comparatively recent times. While the universities in the North battled throughout some of the darkest years of the 'Troubles', they did not make (and have not made) any direct social intervention. Instead, they went quietly and methodically about their business of producing a generation of bright, knowledgeable and hopeful students, the majority of whom left the North for work elsewhere. Similarly, the second level of education, the schools, were at the very cutting edge of community conflict. Faced with the experience of trying to keep their pupils and staff in some kind of 'normal' educational environment, while outside the school gates the slogans and violence and relentless noise of conflict raged with riots. The school authorities opted for a 'play-safe' policy and who would blame them?

With political life reduced as it generally was in Northern Ireland throughout the 1970s and '80s to a war of sectarian violence and cultural attrition, the foundation of that civic space essential in a liberal democracy was fragmentary and uncertain. This condition, which many saw as terminal, was of course a legacy of earlier power struggles in the twentieth century.

The most important of these power struggles is now drawing to an end. It is the unhealthy, indeed incestuous, relationship between church and state that gave birth in 1922 to both states, and it was always going to destabilise any concerted attempt to create a vibrant civic society in Ireland, north or south.

The forty-odd years between 1922 and 1968, when civil rights were demanded in the North, were not noted for any such widespread secularising effort to create a pluralist, inclusive liberal federation within Ireland. In what became the Republic of Ireland, the Roman Catholic Church, along with a complicit ruling class, established a state in its own image: profoundly conservative and puritanical on moral and sexual issues, introverted and victorious. This cultural code was to succeed without much opposition (liberals, republicans and socialists were effectively marginalised), probably because the vulnerable economic conditions in mid-century Ireland encouraged public caution, whatever about private realities. The viability of the state depended upon political inertia, and few lasting voices within Ireland rocked the boat.

With the separate development of northern and southern societies, notwithstanding local and continual cross-border contact, cultural and ideological differences inside the country grew into stereotypes which eventually fed back into the eruption of civil unrest and sectarian warfare in the late 1960s and early 1970s. This internal history has yet to be written and the buried prejudices, tacit assumptions, blindnesses and social disharmony that grew out of the partitioned country came to haunt the country with a vengeance. It is obviously through the educational system that such demystification will have to take place. But here we enter into an ideological maze. From which perspective is the past to be viewed?

At ground level, so much is at stake: personal and cultural identity, in effect. And while it is easy to sympathise with those critics and commentators who are sick, sore and tired of 'the Irish problem', and the (wrongly) perceived Irish obsession with 'Irishness', the truth of the matter is that this issue of cultural identity, based upon national self-consciousness, is at the very core of the debate about the kind of civic society Ireland will be in the new century, never mind what kind of society Ireland was in the century just passed.

From the break-up of Yugoslavia, to the divorce of the Czech and Slovak republics, the unravelling of the Soviet Union, the re-emergence of fascism, through to the anti-federalist movement in Italy, towards the anxieties of the Nordic countries about joining the European Union, and the surfacing of deep-seated anti-multiculturalist tensions and possibilities within the British state – all these issues are directly related to the need for 'cultural identity'.

In the specific context of Ireland, the situation is this in a nutshell. As with other countries of the European mainland, Ireland and Britain are having at long last to come to terms with the realities of living between a variable set of cultures – old and traditional, totally different, exciting, unpredictable, unknown, alien. Whether beamed through satellite or experienced at first hand, exposure to this narrowing world's cultural *à la carte* creates all kinds of expectations in a society that is, simultaneously and in fits and starts, *shedding* its paternalistic selves. But, as a society, there is little real understanding of what this means, or where it is leading, culturally and ideologically.

In Ireland the metamorphosis has had some immediate and irreversible effects – from the declaration of the ceasefires in the North to the widespread provision of civic and legal rights, to the increasing numbers of refugees seeking a new life in the country. How this metamorphosis will be reflected in a wider political and social vision, embodied in the educational system, its related pedagogical ideologies, and played out in the symbols and ceremonies of Irish public life, can only be speculated upon. For what constitutes 'Irish' life is still a question of cultural validation and political legitimacy.

'Irish' must, after all, nominate an 'Ireland'. There is also subtextually present in the term 'Irish', the notion of a subject of 'minority' status: an oppressed people read as an unreleased, decolonisable 'self'. Indeed, the notion that Irish *is* a minority underscores, in contradictory ways, Irish Studies, and it has in very recent years, from the late 1980s to the 1990s, found a new rhetoric. As Terence Brown has remarked:

> The use of postcolonial models of cultural development have certainly emphasised Irish particularism, since the concern to establish that Ireland is a postcolonial society, while involving comparisons with other countries on the level of theory and concept, has tended to write Britain out of the equation, or has re-formulated it as an unchanging 'England' with which Ireland has only related as victim or other. The sense of Ireland as somehow kin of other developing countries has been gratifying

on the theoretical and sentimental levels, but has coexisted with a good deal of isolationism. This theoretical and sentimental positioning of Ireland as a postcolonial culture has meant little actual cultural contact with non-European countries, while it has encouraged a lack of interest in the socio/cultural condition of modern Britain. Developments in Scotland and Wales are largely ignored.

The Great Famine of the mid-nineteenth century, visited upon the supine and stateless nation by a vicious and uncaring imperial power, is now being alluded to as Ireland's 'holocaust'; the famine ships which left the country during and since the 1840s summon up the pain and oppressiveness of exile which is now read in contemporary discourse as Ireland's 'diaspora'. The comparison, unstated but dramatically present nonetheless, is with the experience of European Jewry and with Third World non-metropolitan countries. Terry Eagleton points out:

> 'Ireland' means, romantically, a 'way of life' – means 'culture' in a sense that 'Bolivianness' doesn't, particularly for Anglo-Saxons – and a body of distinguished literary work couched, conveniently enough, in the dominant world language. Equally, the ideological category of Irishness signifies on the

one hand roots, belonging, tradition,
Gemeinschaft, and, on the other, again with
marvellous convenience, exile, diffusion,
globality, diaspora. As a concept it is thus
particular and universal together, rather
like the classical work of art, or indeed the
migrant subject of the postmodern order.

Categories of study should always be nominal means
of production; not ends in themselves, otherwise they
become iron masks or what Samuel Beckett called
'book-keeping'. Unless it is honestly engaged by the
Britishness of Ireland as much as by its European
dimensions and history, and the significant intercultural
implications of the 'new' Irish, Irish Studies runs the
risk of being a cybernetic recycling plant for historical
navel-gazing. As it stands, the country is awash with
conferences, committees, and summer schools devoted
to Irish identity. But are the categories we have worked
from valid anymore? Ireland, like Britain, is a figment
of all our imaginations: Irish, English, Scottish, Welsh,
European, and a host of other emigrant cultures. And
as Hugh Kearney's marvellous study *The British Isles:
A History of Four Nations* makes abundantly clear,
there is a much more powerful proviso, which should
not under any circumstances be discounted:

By the 1970s throughout the former
British empire, in India, Pakistan, Africa,
and the Far East, it seemed as if British
Isles culture would be mediated through

the United States. Within the British Isles itself, American influence in the form of a military presence, fast-food chains, TV programmes and films continued to grow. To an observer at the end of the twentieth century it might well seem that the various cultures of the British Isles would be submerged in a vast transatlantic cultural aggregation. In such a situation, the 'national' categories of the nineteenth century appear to be of ever-diminishing value to the historian.

So are we all, then – historians, academics, writers, readers – only kidding ourselves with all this endless talk about 'cultural' identity?

In a fascinating anthology, *Extravagant Strangers: A Literature of Belonging*, edited by Caryl Phillips, the understandable and necessary desire to identify the immigrant and outsider experience of Britain, going back two hundred years, not one Irish voice is heard. It is hard to believe, given the known facts of the interrelationship between the two islands, from the early decades of the nineteenth century through the waves of emigration of the 1950s and 1980s, that not one Irish writer is included, from Wilde to Yeats, Elizabeth Bowen to Louis MacNeice, or William Trevor, or the remarkable second-generation Irish writers in Britain.

It is no harm to consider that one of the best-known poems in the English language, 'The Lake Isle of Innisfree', started its life in London's Fleet Street, in mid-winter 1888. The 'first lyric' with Yeats' 'own music', as his *Autobiographies* tell us, sprang from a moment of nostalgia when a fountain in a shop window caught Yeats' attention and he 'began to remember lake water'.

Graham Greene's novel *The Third Man* not only anticipated the contemporary fluidity of literary form – film as novel – it also showed how Greene dramatised history as both education and entertainment. As this most European of English writers demonstrates, the artistic imagination can only be conditioned but not limited by ideological (or pedagogically consoling) boundaries. Any writer worth his or her salt repeatedly assails and subverts these boundaries, using whatever language is at their command, in whatever cultural frame they may be most at home in, hostile to, or troubled by. All the best editorial and critical will in the world to lock the writer in a box labelled 'English', 'Irish' or 'Anglo-Irish', or whatever, is pie in the sky. As Holly Martins says in *The Third Man*, 'What do you mean *put*? I don't want to put anybody anywhere.'

1998

CHAPTER NINE

CULTURAL RESOLUTION

'I only know the city of my childhood, I
must have seen the other, but unbelieving.
All I say cancels out, I'll have said nothing.'

Samuel Beckett, 'The Calmative'

I worked as a temporary postman when I was a
student in the late 1960s and early '70s. The job, which
I enjoyed immensely, opened my eyes to a Belfast I
had never really seen before. It was Christmas. I
brought letters and small parcels to back streets in
both Protestant and Catholic areas. In some I saw, for
the first time, real poverty. I could hardly believe it.
Years later I read about the Blitz in Belfast in 1941 and
the reaction of many country folk to the evacuated
children who stayed with them. They couldn't believe
their eyes either. They had never seen such poverty
before: the undernourished bodies, the hardened
faces; the gallows humour of the gaunt parents. The
country people thought the Belfast people had come

from some other world, speaking a language they couldn't understand. Poor housing, inadequate social amenities, this was an unconnected underclass in Belfast, who had been marginalised and somehow had to survive in such conditions for the better part of twenty-five years between the late 1940s and the 1960s. The churches languished; the state ignored; the people lived and died. We all know what happened in the following twenty-five years as the city slipped incrementally into violence and strife. Estates became small towns of their own with their own 'police', codes and social structure and the life was more or less sucked out of Belfast city centre. With such a history, it's hardly surprising that the cultural life of post-war Belfast has been chequered, to put it at its mildest.

Culture was a possession, politically validated as 'national' identity, on the one hand, or anxiously transcendent, on the other. While the middle class took its artistic bearings from London (less so from Dublin), the landowning class displayed little interest. Between them, local cultural expression – in terms of literary or dramatic art – was left to look after itself as best it could.

For a brief period during the 1960s the city witnessed a kind of artistic flourishing. Newspapers such as the *Belfast Telegraph* devoted pages to local writing and the music scene blossomed. Queen's University looked beyond its own walls and established a festival and publishing imprint, and throughout the city festivals of one kind or another prospered, including the Falls Fleadh. But the ensuing years of 'the Troubles' stunted these developments or shattered them. Now that the political barometer is on the up again, it is hardly surprising that the issue of Belfast's cultural life is resurfacing. But the first question that comes to mind is whether or not 'Belfast' exists any more as a city. Is Belfast now not much more than a geographical mosaic that has spread haphazardly up and away from the central thoroughfares and arterial roads into massed compass points such as west Belfast – a city more or less on its own? What connectedness west Belfast has with the rest of the city is a critical point. And what of the numerous estates, villages in themselves, that seem to shun the outside world with their martial archways of entry and commemorative murals and their own way of life lived inside swathes of green playing fields which shoulder the forbidding motorways?

Has anyone asked how the people who live in these districts feel about Belfast? Does anyone care? It is also worthwhile questioning what is meant by 'culture' in Belfast. There was once deep discomfort with the term when it was applied to popular forms of expression, such as band and choral music or traditional Irish dance and music. In more recent years Belfast's cultural 'roots' in the global British imperial project of the late nineteenth and early twentieth centuries (the industrial, maritime and technological heritage of the city) have become problematical. Historical realities can complicate current political exigencies and insist upon a kind of cultural forgetting. Discomfort with the Gaelic palimpsest of the city, from the named landscape to parts of speech and the hinterland of our self-consciousness, has been overcome. In no small part this has been due to the innovative and ground-breaking foundational work in the 1970s of Michael Longley in the Arts Council and a little earlier of David Hammond and Douglas Carson, among others, working in the BBC. These and others broke down the political barriers between past and present and made a common culture visible to all those in Belfast who were truly interested in discovering their city. The trouble is with the future meaning of the city and what it stands for in cultural terms. Before that debate is engaged in, it is imperative to clear out of the way the tired old harangue about 'popular' versus 'elitist'. It is the marriage of the best of both that creates imaginative energy, and anything which achieves that should be welcomed. Self-regarding dogmas about 'identity' have to go. They appeal to the notion that art can do things it was never meant to do. In a time of shocking upheaval and disturbance, many felt that 'the arts' should respond more directly to the search for resolution. That is no longer the case. The reconciliation business should be left to get on with its own agenda. Politically inspired orthodoxies that insist upon 'the arts' serving this community or that (while the writer functions as spokesperson) produce little of lasting artistic worth. The temptation to see the arts as a significant (substitute) part of cultural tourism also must be watched like a hawk. But these are in many ways abstract points when placed in the context of the much more pressing issues of a radical re-evaluation of arts policy. Is the integration of the estates and physically segregated districts into an overall sense of Belfast a realistic option? Do people see Belfast as their capital in any meaningful way, a place to which they owe a sense of belonging over and above local political bonds of district and neighbourhood? Before these issues can be tackled, Belfast needs a vision of and for itself. A physical architectural plan, a civic vision, if you like, with which its citizens – the long resident and the recently arrived migrant workers – can feel at home. In the absence of such a planned vision, the arts will be looked at, under political duress, for all the wrong reasons: easy pickings, lip service, are phrases that come to mind.

A good start – if it hasn't already happened – would be to establish an independent civic forum for those who have a personal and professional interest in 'promoting' the arts in Belfast. Most of all, Belfast needs the dynamic younger generation of, among others, entrepreneurs, actors, architects, musicians, visual artists and writers to engage with the city. The unshackling of the political jockeys who ride every cultural identity horse is a basic requirement, whether that be the 'Ulster Scots' project which threatens to overload a valuable, human resource with historically attenuated significance and political freight, or the mandatory 'Irishness' which smothers so much that is intuitive and various in Belfast's cultural life.

Social engineering underpins cultural apartheid; it doesn't transform it. It may produce an audience but it will not challenge that audience to think critically about its own inherited way of thinking. And it is precisely this dynamic and critically open drive that Belfast, like Northern Ireland, needs, not recycling the old, tried and tested routes. But 'culture', particularly literature, and the recognition of its artistic value, as much as its civic function, sits uneasily in Northern society. No one can be in any doubt about the difficulties Belfast faces in coming to terms with its past. Name one other western European city since World War II which has had to accept the fact that a significant minority of its citizens (the terrorists of both sides) dedicated their adult lives to destroying the place one way or another – and inflicting, during twenty-five years, untold suffering on hundreds of thousands of their fellow citizens. This reality has kept parts of ourselves locked up in a state of disbelief. Others have 'moved on', effectively in a condition of denial, towards an ethical zone of collective blamelessness; others again created a language of military self-regard to inoculate themselves from the messy and ugly reality of the brutally inept campaign of violence which saw innocent civilians pay the ultimate price in vastly greater numbers than the so-called 'soldiers'.

Putting all this aside, however, and looking to the future, and the role that 'the arts' might play in the recovery of Northern society, an obvious point first. Surely it's about time for the city 'fathers' to catch themselves on and engage with 'the arts', seeking serious funding from the public and private sectors. Rather than believing that cultural priorities and the procedures for adjudicating them should be imported, the real challenge is to finance and nurture individual talent and resources in Belfast and develop a coherent civic programme of excellence based in the capital city.

Maybe, though, I am afflicted with nostalgia and the mistaken belief that there can ever be a reconstructed cultural sense of Belfast. Not because there isn't the will to source a cultural inclusivity, but rather because Belfast, like other post-industrial cities in Britain and Ireland, is no longer a collective homogeneous space. Instead, it is a series of ideas and histories of communities, some of which intersect and have creative potential; others do not and are merely reproduced as consoling (political or social) fictions. Belfast, in this sense, does not exist because the people do not have a shared, generally accepted sense of what the place means. It may also be the case that the traditional status of the cultural activity I have been describing is becoming a thing of the past anyway and that creative energy is much more drawn in general away from literature to film and global 'pop' culture.

If Belfast is a patchwork of different places, districts and neighbourhoods hostile to and marooned from one another, it's likely that vested interests will resist any 'unifying' consciousness, political as much as cultural. And if arts organisations and festivals are funded on sectional interests, then clearly there is little reason to change. The industrial, commercial and historical experience that kept the city together, in often intimate adversity, no longer holds sway. The key question in all this is what will fill that void if

Belfast is seen merely as a place one passes through on the way home. It could be anywhere else in the UK with its architectural character blurred into meaninglessness. What proportion there was to the centre of the city and what could have been built upon its remaining physical matrix – realigned with a little imaginative effect – has been, at best, overlooked; at worse, flattened or raised into banal anonymous modernity. Between the Linen Hall Library, a model for the future, if ever there were one, and the Odyssey and Waterfront, landmark breaks from the past, the cultural life of the city can be reclaimed as a thriving city for people to live in once again and to share, with a feeling of belonging, fearlessness and pride. Or is that too much to ask?

2003

CHAPTER TEN

Unhealthy
Intersections

In 1983 Eavan Boland's review of a series of
pamphlets published by Field Day, referred to at the
beginning of this book, she remarked that 'if the new
nationalism' being proposed 'contained all the voices,
all the fragments, all the dualities and ambiguities
of reference', she would welcome it, 'but it doesn't'.
She went on: 'Judging by the ... pamphlets ... this is
green nationalism and divided culture,' before quoting
Derek Mahon's point that 'Whatever we mean by the
Irish situation, the shipyards of Belfast are no less a
part of it than a country town in the Gaeltacht'. Forty
years later the shipyards have gone and are now a
hugely popular tourist attraction for the *Titanic*, while
the long-term future of the Gaeltacht shrinks and
grows more vulnerable. The 'new nationalism' which
Field Day had sought to inspire and encourage debate
about in the 1980s and '90s was a response to the
political and social crisis of Northern Irish society, a

crisis that had spilled with lethal effect over into the rest of Ireland, Britain and elsewhere. Debates and political pressure surrounded the notion of the writer in Ireland throughout the 1980s and centred mainly on the role and responsibility of the writer, who was seen as a kind of weathervane for the legacies of inherited conflict over cultural identity. Thankfully, much water has gone under those bridges since the negotiated resolution of the conflict with the Good Friday Agreement in 1998 and the period of relative peace that has followed from it. The 'reconciliation' chimed with developments in Britain and Ireland as the then 'new' governments of Blair and Ahern took advantage of an improving economic climate to boost the optimism of the young ('Things will only get better').

The infamous Celtic Tiger had started to roar and, with it, society in the Republic became switched off from the politics of the past. The economy boomed. For the first time in its history, the Republic experienced the heady brew of sky-high property prices and wealth on an unprecedented scale.

With an immigrant population swelling the state's reserves, the transformation of Irish society into a multi-cultural secular democracy seemed inevitable; at ease with its neighbours, mixing it up with the best of them under the lax tax regimes of an indulgent government, taking its cue from property developers, bankers and corporate managers. The party would last for ever we were led to believe; which of course it didn't.

But now that the 'economic nationalism' of the Celtic Tiger is in tatters, these comparisons are curiously apt because the writer is once again being asked to perform his/her patriotic duty as part of the expectation raised in various quarters, that culture and 'the Arts' in Ireland will, and should, ride to the rescue of an incompetent state and the exploitative class of bankers and others who squandered the resources of the boom, having first lavishly secured their own futures while bequeathing to the taxpayer the cost of the bailout. This is a political problem that needs decisive action on economic and fiscal matters for the next quarter of a century. It has got nothing whatsoever to do with writing. The balm that cultural tourism brings should not be seen as anything other than a diplomatic boost to help things along; it is certainly no substitute for or solution to the abject failures of the economic and political system in Ireland in recent years.

Writers are being co-opted into a script of national idealism and self-centredness that recalls the response to the Northern crisis of the Troubles. Linked to the belief that the image of Ireland has been tarnished by the commercial and financial chicanery of a few, it was inevitable that some revival of nationalism was on the cards. The real question is – what will this actually achieve? More specifically, what does it mean for our literary culture to become too aligned with, perhaps indebted to, the current immediacies of politically expedient agendas?

The actual tradition of Irish writers from the eighteenth century to the late twentieth century is generally one of artistic defiance and imaginative challenge, rather than one of cultural compliance and orthodoxy. We shouldn't discount as inconvenient Beckett's dismissive letter of January 1938 – in response to his good friend, the poet and one-time director of the National Gallery of Ireland, Thomas MacGreevy's essay on Jack Yeats. Beckett confesses to a 'chronic inability to understand ... a phrase like "the Irish people", or to imagine it ever gave a fart in its corduroys ... for any form of art whatsoever ... or that it will ever care, if it ever knows, any more than the Bog of Allen will ever care or know, that there was once a painter in Ireland called Jack Butler Yeats'.

Writers have always had a complicatedly intimate relationship with the Irish state – one prominent writer spoke recently of his 'shame' at what was happening, a noteworthy personalising of the economic situation. People in Ireland, and Irish people outside the country, justly take pride and self-confidence in the achievements of Irish writing on the world stage. But we also have to recognise that the great twentieth-century writers from Ireland – to take these as an example – had contradictory relationships with the Irish state and its ruling ideologies. Just think of Joyce, or Kavanagh, or Bowen, or McGahern as examples. As writers, each of them saw their work in the comparative context of other European and American writers, not in terms of how they *felt* about the place they came from – which was much too important an emotional connection to be exploited. Indeed, the notion of feeling 'passionate' about things has itself become a meaningless cliché.

Part of the problem the country has faced in the outworking of the political and cultural period of the Celtic Tiger is that relatively little was learned from other economies which had experienced a similar rapid boom. No plans were put in place to secure the economic gains. And the class spread of the wealth was patchy at best. One need only look at how exposed the working-class estates are throughout the country to drugs, social disorder and dismembering violence. The sense of apprehension in the night streets has become so customary that people accept it as a fact of life in Irish towns and cities.

The aesthetic impoverishment of so many of these places, along with large swathes of the countryside, sits bizarrely alongside the (by now) expired portrait of an Ireland as visually alert and committed to preserving what was best in the landscape, not destroying it. Yet the organs of the state and local governance simply were not fit for purpose or powerful enough to protect that landscape from greedy developers. As Fintan O'Toole remarked with an exasperation close to despair, 'You have to be in awe of a ruling class that can use its incompetence to escape the consequences of its incompetence.' In these circumstances, 'awe' may not be quite the right word.

In the years ahead, others will sift through the published literature to see which were the achieved works carrying imaginative challenge and historical veracity to future generations. The immediate post-Tiger years will probably slip into history and the culpability and mismanagement visited upon the country by the financial and political elite – with no ability of our own to seek recompense – will fade too, leaving in its wake the fiction that Ireland, while being culturally exceptional, is/was economically unmanned by all-powerful global forces beyond its/our control. Ownership of a recession is clearly a mug's game.

Piety now raises its head where once there had been gung-ho speculators – in real estate as much as in cultural chutzpah. As John McGahern wrote of the 1950s, a much more difficult time than the present, 'pious humbug often afflicts the Arts'. Indeed, McGahern's beloved Kavanagh didn't put a tooth in it in his *Self Portrait*:

> For twenty years I wrote according to the dispensation of this Irish school. The appraisers of the school all agreed that I had my roots in the soil, was one of the people and that I was an authentic voice. What the alleged poetry lover loved was the Irishness of a thing. Irishness is a form of anti-art. A way of posing as a poet without actually being one.

It simply is not 'healthy', as a younger contemporary writer has put it, 'for the cultural life of a country for the artists to be cosying up with the political elite and brand "Ireland".' Whatever about their beliefs and actions as citizens, this kind of expectation for writers is, as Conor Cruise O'Brien once had it, an unhealthy intersection. Remember Louis MacNeice's injunction from the 1930s: 'The writer today should be not so much the mouthpiece of a community (for he will only tell it what it knows already) as its conscience, its critical faculty, its generous instinct.'

Maybe in the decades ahead literary and cultural comparisons will be made with countries similar to our own. Rather than the dreamtime of a very old kind of soft-centred nationalism, what is needed now is an outward-looking, clear-sighted and buoyant appreciation of where we are in the world. A practical vision based upon the country's maritime and agricultural roots, committed to new 'green' technologies, mindful of our exceptional literary and cultural achievements, alongside the physical distinctiveness of the landscape. With its contradictory and varied history and long-standing ties to Britain, Europe and the US, Ireland is a *unique* island of the in between, and nowhere more so than Belfast.

When I am back there, I often take myself and the dog for a walk along the Lagan towpath. It's a beautiful place of silence but for the sounds of birdlife and the river flowing in from the bog meadows. Lighters used this canal way to take produce and material to and from Belfast's harbour, and the remains of this old transport system are still present here and there as a reminder of a previous way of life, previous, that is, to the great industrial history of the city that has itself largely become a thing of the past.

As a boy growing up in the 1950s, the city was simply *defined* by its industrial life. The smells, the sirens, the shipping, the Scottish Gothic architecture of the insurance houses and banks, the commercial and manufacturing that was at the heart of Belfast experience, shaped everything from streetscape to skyline. Yet country life in Belfast was never that far away – in the surrounding hills and meadows, in the proximity to the coastline and in the presence of the rivers like the Lagan, and in the parks, gardens and groves that are inscribed like pleasure grounds within the red brick avenues and busy thoroughfares.

Thirty years ago you wouldn't have dared take a walk along those towpaths for fear of what you might come across. Belfast in the 1970s, '80s and early '90s was a city at war with itself, and the damage those years caused to the ordinary people remains, not so visibly but inwardly. The city itself has moved on because it had to. The young don't look back and those in their middle years and older seem to have made a pact with themselves that the city can't and won't let itself return to the bad old days of the Troubles, which is not to say that everything is right with the city. It isn't.

The peace walls of steel girders that slice their way through local inner-city neighbourhoods are dreadful physical reminders of the divisions within the community and of how people have accepted as best as anyone can that these ugly scars of sectarianism just haven't gone away. Nor can the moral and emotional turmoil of so much violence and damage simply be dismissed with pious gestures. Listen to the talk shows. At some deep level the reality of what was done in the years of the Troubles has found no common civic understanding because those involved still don't really *see* the damage, and probably never will.

Unlike Dublin and many other cities in the Republic, Belfast survived the Celtic Tiger because it wasn't centrally a part of it. Maybe the ostentatious displays of wealth sat less comfortably in a city that has known boom and bust over many generations of economic hardship and revival. The UK-subsidised economy of the North, and none more so than in Belfast, has learnt how to steady itself with entrepreneurial and commercial *nous* that has often been caricatured as canny, when others might applaud it as cautious – but then just look at what the gung-ho Irish bankers and property dealers brought upon all our heads.

Belfast is enjoying being itself again. The hotels, restaurants and bars, so far as one can ever tell, are doing well; the writers, musicians and artists are going about their business with unassuming diligence and success. The art galleries, theatres and drama groups are active, along with the handful of local publishers and the festivals and concert venues are all producing first-rate events for their constituencies while battling like everyone else on the sponsorship front. The streets are swept. You see folks lying out in the sun on the lawns around the impressively refurbished City Hall, as if it was the mid-sixties all over again, except for the enormous screen for transmitting concerts. And the school kids in their different uniforms head home at the same time as they've always done. And people look you straight in the eye as if you or they were about to ask a question.

So in the morning I head off along the Lagan and past the wonderful new Lyric Theatre. In my mind the connection to the Lyric goes back to the 1960s when, along with other friends at Orangefield School, I was involved in the Lyric Youth Theatre. In those days the group met in a church hall in Cromwell Road, a Judith-Hearne-like street just off Belfast's Botanic Avenue.

In that hall we were instructed to dance by the wonderful Helen Lewis, author of the Holocaust memoir *A Time to Speak*, and in theatre practice by Sam McCready, a powerhouse of dramatic proportions. With the O'Malley family, the Lyric's founders, and many other local theatre people, Sam bridged the generations and linked the upcoming younger generation with the established Lyric in its 'then' new home on Ridgeway Street in south Belfast.

Nestled inside the rising redbrick streetscape above the Lagan River, and under the busy suburban thoroughfare of Stranmillis, the theatre found a home for itself nearby the College of Education, the Ulster Museum, Queen's University and the Botanic Gardens. The Lyric in the sixties was a little out of Belfast city centre's self-consciousness but it was to become a great beacon of hope and perseverance during the very dark days when Belfast plummeted into the Troubles.

As bombing, gunfire, curfews and mayhem engulfed the inner city, the theatre refused to close its doors. In a sense the theatre, stage, foyer and surroundings seemed to be somewhat like a secular church, no matter what play there was in performance. The Lyric had a battle to survive not just the local violence of the times but also the struggle that all theatres experience working through difficult contemporary commercial challenges and cultural changes.

When my mother and stepfather moved in retirement to south Belfast, my returns home often included a walk along the neighbouring Lagan via Annadale and the allotments. The Lyric sat across the riverbank, looking increasingly more isolated and bruised as the houses around Ridgeway Street lost their residents and turned increasingly into rented accommodation. Almost a sense of foreboding descended. Despite all the pleasure and tribulation overcome in the theatre's past, the Lyric looked isolated. For a city not greatly given to civic appreciation of its literary cultural legacy, never mind making much effort to promote the diverse success of its artistic community over several generations, the new Lyric that has stepped out from behind the scaffolding is a brave and defiant statement of belief in the future, not least for the dramatic arts in Belfast. My hope is that the theatre will be able to integrate itself much more dynamically with the Belfast that is emerging out of the heavy industrial past. It would be great too if the new Lyric could re-establish itself firmly and coherently in its rich cultural roots in Irish theatre as well as welcoming the best of work from Britain and further afield.

Now reimagined as a prominent light-filled, outward-looking auditorium, the Lyric is no longer metaphorically hidden within the rocky hillside of Ridgeway Street, but rather stands out, like the prow of a ship. As the young women and men go out jogging, no matter what the weather's like, running without fear, I can't help thinking that that spirit, if it keeps going, is the real symbolic shape-changer – before which much else is possible, not just in Belfast, of course, but on the island of Ireland as a whole.

2011–15

CHAPTER ELEVEN

The Hand of History

On 23 May 2016, in a series called 'Behind the Headlines', the Long Room Hub, the arts and humanities research centre at Trinity College Dublin, hosted a discussion on Brexit, a full month before the referendum took place (23 June). I was one of the speakers, my task to reflect on the long journey towards peace in Northern Ireland and how Brexit could jeopardise this. But I was also asked to think about the use of language in the debate surrounding Brexit and what could be interpreted as 'unforeseen consequences' – the title of my short paper.

My co-speakers included the then British Ambassador to Ireland, Dominick Chilcott, Dr Etain Tannam, a lecturer in Peace Studies at Trinity, Professor Eunan O'Halpin, director of the Trinity Centre of Contemporary Irish History (and an authority on political and diplomatic relations between Ireland and Britain), and in the chair was Professor Jane Ohlmeyer, author of the major study *Making Ireland English: The Irish Aristocracy in the Seventeenth Century*.

The reason why I'm bothering with these local details is to illustrate a simple initial point – that the panel taking part in that discussion was taking the subject very seriously, if not in a sombre mood, and so doing, even though the actual referendum was in another country in which we had no vote, except, that is, for the Ambassador.

The Thomas Davis Lecture Theatre was packed to capacity with over two hundred people, many of them young and, as we would hear in the discussion, many were English living in Ireland, and some Irish living in Britain. In one contribution, an English visitor to Dublin who was passing through and heard about the debate and simply dropped by, asked: 'Why are we not having this kind of discussion back in Britain; it's so refreshing to hear this in place of the rancour at home'. Or words to that effect. So there we were, a month before the referendum and this is what I said:

> Eighteen years ago the Good Friday Agreement, which was overwhelmingly endorsed by the people in Ireland, put paid to a very dark and bitter quarter of a century of violence and political acrimony that we have consigned to history as 'the Troubles'. It's hardly feasible to think today that in the late 1960s a democratic movement for civil rights would spiral out of control from street protest and popular demands for economic and cultural justice

into such a shocking conflict between terrorism and state force that would lead to the deaths of thousands of ordinary men, women and children. We know this story well and I'm not going to rehearse it tonight save to make the simple point that behind the protracted discussions, arguments, debates and difficulties of the years since, the Good Friday Agreement has set a generation largely free from violence, both physical and verbal. My fear is that this hard-won and costly political achievement could unravel at the behest of what is increasingly being seen as an incoherent, ill-conceived and, at times, nasty racist debate about Brexit. At the heart of this debate there seems to be a serious and potentially hugely damaging ignorance about what might happen should the British electorate decide to leave the European Union. Listen to what Lord Lawson, the chairman of the 'Vote Leave' campaign, had to say on the Andrew Marr Show (BBC, 10 April 2016) about the issue of frontier controls and custom checks, i.e. the international border that would be put in place between the EU and the UK, a border that would run across the northern counties of Ireland: Derry, Fermanagh, Tyrone, Armagh and Down/ Louth, Monaghan, Leitrim, Cavan and

Donegal: 'checks would be needed along the Border to prevent illegal immigration. That could be stopped. There would have to be border controls, but not a prevention of genuine Irish coming in.'

There would be, I guess, forty or so crossing points – what used to be known as 'unapproved roads' – in the interface between Louth and Down. So do the maths and you can begin to see the farce this is all leading to, not to mention the phrase of letting the 'genuine Irish coming in'. With a shillelagh under me arm, no doubt, and a twinkle in me eye. The lack of basic historical knowledge is baffling but clearly self-serving. Another government campaigner for the Leave side, Dominic Raab, is reported as saying (in an interview with Dermot Murnaghan, Sky News, 11 April 2016) that Brexit could see 'an end to the open border between the two parts of Ireland' and he is quoted as boldly stating, rather awkwardly: 'If you're worried about border controls and security … you couldn't leave a back door without some kind, either of checks there with any country or assurances in relation to the checks that they're conducting, obviously. Otherwise, everyone with ill will towards this country [UK] would go round that route.'

'Obviously' isn't really the word; it defies logic that anyone with a titter of wit would know that the border in Ireland has been for almost one hundred years a scar on the body politic which we have only very recently started to heal with the balm of common sense and years of very hard work on the ground.

To retreat from this still delicately balanced issue because you are ensconced in the internal battles for the high ground of your political party and like the sound of your own voice, is utterly foolhardy and irresponsible.

But Brexit isn't about Ireland. And wouldn't be, were it not for the 'special relationship' between the various parts of these islands and not just Ireland and Britain. Indeed I'm not even sure, after all is said and done, if Brexit is not actually about a deepening sense of disaffection with itself, particularly in mainstream *English* society.

The driving force behind Brexit is London-based power politics. What happens in Jonesborough or Forkhill or Pettigo is a very long way away. And that's exactly the mistake that could come to haunt this referendum. But there is also a very troubling element to the language of the debate in England. From an outsider's point of view, I am shaken by the toxic and dangerous racist element that leading figures of the Leave side introduced into what should be a lively and important democratic debate.

It staggers belief to think how phrases like 'genuine Irish' are used so casually or the hugely publicised doubts expressed by the ex-mayor of London about the racial origins of Barack Obama's opinions on Brexit or the shameful comparison by the ex-mayor of London, of EU bureaucrats with Hitler and the Nazi Third Reich's destruction of Europe.

What would have played out if similar terms had been hurled about publicly in the hothouse of Northern Irish parliamentary debate is difficult to imagine. But perhaps it is, from this distance, the lack of a robust civic leadership surrounding the referendum that could well produce unforeseen circumstances – something we will all have to deal with for years to come and I'm not just talking about the murky aftermath of a resurrected border in Ireland. The snide innuendos of a 'Little Englander' nostalgia for imperial grandeur, mocked-up by so-called plain-speaking ordinary blokes who tell it like it is, need to be challenged by mature and reasonable arguments.

For, as we know, there are important matters at stake here – about security and immigration, integration and civil rights; but also about bureaucratic power and the deepening suspicions of a European elite as self-perpetuating. However, the maturity and experience that even a little history brings to the table would help, rather than so much bluff and bluster that the 'Leave' campaign is leaving in its wake.

The Republic of Ireland joined up to Europe almost fifty years ago. If there is an alternative in the next fifty years for these islands, then spell it out. Let's hear how we can do business differently, politically, economically, culturally. I doubt there is such a rationale. But the one thing that is becoming increasingly more obvious is that the current Leave campaign is sounding strident, silly, contradictory and ill-informed on what exactly will happen should their campaign succeed. If however we repeat some very dangerous mistakes from the past, particularly in the way we address each other – that, in anyone's language, could spell disaster.

That was the speech and a short time later it surfaced in a slightly revised and retrospective version in a pamphlet, *English after Brexit*, along with contributions from among others, poet and scholar Peter Robinson, edited by the distinguished academic Adrian Barlow and published by the English Association. I would like to revisit some of the points I touched upon there, considering what it looks like as an outsider who is currently and temporarily living in what will eventually be 'Brexitland'. I'd also like to register as best I can and as good-heartedly as possible, my responses to what happened, and is happening, between the referendum decision of last summer and roughly how things look today.

This is not an academic paper but a gathering of anecdotes and impressions which record my own struggle to find some kind of intellectual bearing on where we – or maybe that should be 'you' – are presently as a culture; a culture that heavily influenced my own educational and moral upbringing in post-war Belfast of the 1950s and '60s.

That I spent a good bit of time during the late 1980s, 1990s and early years of this century in various parts of Europe, giving poetry readings and lectures and attending conferences, including in the former eastern European countries, and that as an Irish citizen I am and will remain, as my passport says in Irish, part of 'An tAontas Eorpach' – a member of the European Union – all this will strongly influence what follows. It will probably come as little surprise that I'll be drawing attention to the critical presence of George Orwell and in particular one of his greatest essays, 'Politics and the English Language', written over seventy years ago and published in 1946, as Britain was stabilising itself after the wreckage of World War II and facing into questioning realignments with leading world powers, including the US and, of course, the Soviet Union. The 'present political chaos' Orwell wrote back then, 'is connected with the decay of language, and that one can probably bring about some improvement by starting at the verbal end'.

There is little point in my rehearsing the specific arguments of the Brexit debate here; suffice to say that on any level of detail they have melted into the abstract and, as Orwell remarks: 'no one seems able to think of turns of speech that are not hackneyed: prose consists less and less of *words* chosen for the sake of their meaning, and more and more of *phrases* tacked together like the sections of a prefabricated hen-house'.

Language, Orwell asserted, 'becomes ugly and inaccurate because our thoughts are foolish, but the slovenliness of our language makes it easier for us to have foolish thoughts'.

As Dennis Kennedy, former deputy editor of *The Irish Times*, stated recently, 'to keep repeating "Brexit means Brexit" and "the people have spoken" when we still have no clear idea of what it will really mean, is inane and irresponsible'. Indeed, the fact that we are no wiser on the strategy to extricate Britain from its almost half-century within the European Community makes it all the more baffling to note the democratic passivity that has followed in the wake of the referendum recommendation.

What strikes me most forcibly, however, has been the continuing *tone* of the discussions. The noxious quality of so much that was said in the media is now merging more and more into the fabric of mainstream public discourse in a fashion that is unimaginable to one who has witnessed the so-called 'populism' at first hand in the bigoted language that fueled much of the Northern Irish conflict.

There is nothing 'funny' about Nigel Farage and his side-kicks, who remind me so much of the sectarian bully-boys of the past, that to pretend, as David Cameron did, that these people were in some way 'beneath him' was a fatal error which led indirectly to Cameron's failure in the referendum gamble. It also exposed the complacency and arrogance of those in Britain who thought they had the referendum in the bag.

They didn't, as we know, because the co-called lower orders were beavering away, with a class-based, or class-inflected sense of grievance in their hearts, funded seriously by various business and political interests with their own targeted objectives, and not some ill-defined 'cultural' vision that 'being European' was 'better'. In not getting into this rough-house side of the debate, Labour's failure, or so it seems from the outside, was sealed.

But what catches me out more and more, now that I'm living in the Republic of Ireland when I listen to the strident tones of the Leave faction in government, is just how insecure they are about what they are actually doing. It brings to mind the bluster of the Thatcherite Tory past of the 1980s and the disasters that befell ordinary folk from their blundering and incoherent ideological decision-making, including the juvenile shadow-boxing and shape-throwing of anti-EC (as it then was) posturing.

The infamous early rejection by Thatcher in 1983/84 of the New Ireland Forum and Irish prime minister Garret FitzGerald's proposals for Northern Ireland: 'Out', 'Out', 'Out', only to concede and shape and sign up for the Anglo-Irish Agreement in 1985, comes to mind; the Poll Tax debacle of 1989/90 which led ultimately to Thatcher's fall from power; the repeated denials of culpability surrounding Bloody Sunday; the dire failure of British diplomacy regarding the Hunger Strikes in 1980/81 which led directly to the revitalisation of the IRA campaign and another fifteen years of shocking violence.

Not much here to inspire one with confidence in the Conservative Party's ability to negotiate its way out of a wet paper bag, never mind the complicated labyrinths of EU legislation and commercial relations of five decades. The question that was not asked, and has *not* been asked (possibly for patriotic reasons), is stark enough: which diplomatic or political initiative, undertaken by a Conservative government in the period of EU membership, offers outstanding proof of its collective ability to provide a positive outcome for post-Brexit Britain? Notwithstanding all the huff and puff of economic shackles being unbound, is there unimpeachable evidence that Britain will reclaim some Valhalla of economic prosperity denied to it by ill-disposed Brussels mandarins? Does anyone seriously believe this to be the case?

I have spent many years in the company of Europeans from all over the continent, from smaller countries to the leading and larger, who revere this country and its culture and history; none are impressed by the egotism of some misfiring politicians or the grand-standing of zealots, but that is the case with their own who act in this fashion throughout Europe. There is a sense that Brexit, which has not happened yet, could enter into the lists of Tory disasters unless parliament doesn't become much more active alongside the wider civil society. Certainly, from an outsider's point of view, it appeared that Farage was the leader of a powerful body of opinion in Westminster and not the one-time leader of his ex-party that boasts one MP!

The nasty language of racism and the voicing of religious prejudice that are now becoming authorised in part by this referendum is something that multi-cultural Britain has to challenge much more coherently. Incitement to hatred is incitement to hatred when all is said and done. Orwell again: 'When the general atmosphere is bad, language must suffer ... But if thought corrupts language, language can also corrupt thought.'

For instance, it is pointless merely referring to 'waves of reaction' or 'the rise of populism' spreading across Europe or in the US as some kind of automaton-like mantra. To 'think clearly', Orwell reminds us, 'is a necessary first step towards political regeneration: so that the fight against bad English is not frivolous and is not the exclusive concern of professional writers'.

The Brexit row has done certain good if it has alerted people to what lies under the surface of this society but this awareness cannot be revoked from the outside. This brings me to a very curious point about the extent to which outside knowledge, advice and/or witness were *not* included in the run-up to and post-Brexit discussions. The negativity surrounding the very term 'Europe' and 'European' is noticeable to anyone less invested in the cultural stereotypes of England and the English.

The coverage of the BBC is a case in point. Nightly news stories referring to the *European* 'refugee' crisis involving Syria, Afghanistan and other war-ravaged societies, overlook the fact that this is a *humanitarian* disaster that has produced, though stretched to breaking point, the best of heroic efforts of both Greek and Italian medical and defence forces, aided by fellow EU countries such as Ireland. But somehow this is being seen as 'their' (EU) problem.

Conversely, on a totally different and trivial level entirely, a news item enthusiastically refers to how a young and promising English-born footballer might well leave the Premier League because of lucrative offers from 'the continent', not 'Europe' mark you! Notwithstanding the tosh of 23 June being a British Independence Day, the referendum did produce a curate's egg of a result. Douglas Kennedy: 'in a Vote for leave, only 38% of "the people" (the total electorate) voted to leave, with about 34% to remain. Does that in itself constitute a mandate for the biggest constitutional change in 43 years?' *Discuss*!

Certain matters *are* clear all these months after the vote. 'Following Brexit' as a phrase used in ongoing reference to Britain's economic performance is wrong. Brexit hasn't happened. A referendum on leaving the EU has taken place but the actual reality of Britain not being in the European Union has emphatically not yet been felt yet the media and others continue to maintain the fiction that it has; but so what? Who really cares if the British union breaks up, leaving in its wake four relatively distinct nations to get on as best as they can with one another?

England will continue as England in some form or another. Its role on the world stage that some fantasise about – particularly the series of failed Tory leaders and/or previous (failed) contenders who are 'manning up' the Brexit-side – will be predicated upon the unfolding saga on the other side of the Atlantic and the drip-drip of further revelations about Russia's revivified influence in English and North American politics, all in an effort to undermine the powerful democratic community of European nations.

You can play with that scenario in as many different ways as you like but what cannot be gainsaid is the absolute and clear failure of the English governing class to *plan* for post-referendum Britain. There was no Plan A, never mind a Plan B. Where this leaves the relatively undernourished issue of intellectual and cultural debate in this democracy is hard to know. Language and self-image in political life has merged into the corporate world of media to such an extent that even an abusive use as an electioneering poster of the dire plight of thousands of Syrian families escapes any legal or moral censure.

Outrage at such conduct does not work; nor irony, nor mocking. There is no shortcut but hard work on the ground and the implementation of strong and effective legal and legislative recourse to the courts to clear (at least from the public airwaves) the dog-whistling racism as much as the ranting. The fact that there are two sides (or more) to every negotiating table seems to have simply been erased from public discourse as if 'England' is negotiating with itself and not the actual world. Sound bites and tweets may work for momentary visibility but real people pay at the other end if clearly defined and practical options aren't in place. My gut feeling is that in the present climate and given the current anti-intellectual mood of the country, the promises being stored up *for* and *by* those who voted on an each-way bet that Brexit would give to post-industrial communities a sense of restored dignity and respect, is forlorn. The patronisingly named JAM – just about managing – will not see one iota of improvement as a result of Brexit.

It took about twenty hard years for the Northern peace process to take root and settle in since 1998. There are still tracts of unfulfilled, unfillable wishes and dreams of those who continue to harbour a political return to a past in which they imagined a simpler, changeless life and due comfort. That won't happen, though the occasional spasms of division in Northern Ireland still produce mini-crises. As regards Britain, I can't see where the political and diplomatic experience and intellectual energy is coming from in the present assembly at Westminster or who will provide real leadership for the generation to come, but I hope I'm wrong for all our sakes. On the other hand, things might just muddle along at first, at any rate. Since I've referred to Orwell, let me finish these musings on an Orwellian riff and a nod in the direction of a prediction:

London will become the overall dominant city state with the rest of England and Wales substantially dependent upon its financial services for substantial foreign capital and investment. Scotland will negotiate dual-citizenship with EU membership along with Northern Ireland, as increasingly more people follow the currently high volume of individual applications for Irish nationality (75,000 in the UK in the past six months; and a potential 2.1 million qualify!). Nothing much will have really changed, except for the fact that 'Europe' can no longer be held responsible for any of the economic and/or political challenges/crises that the recalibrated Britain of England and Wales experience. Many universities will announce plans to amalgamate (or face closure) and the elite colleges commit ever more resources to attract highly educated leadership cadres from China, India and other non-EU countries as compensation for Erasmus and equivalent exchanges programmes that have run out of time and funding.

Twenty years from now who can tell what will be the outcome of the Brexit referendum in the UK and whether anything seriously fundamental will have changed in that society for the good of all those who voted either to leave the European Union or to remain. Remember Orwell's injunction – 'to think clearly is a necessary first step towards political regeneration', which is more than enough to be going on with in my book.

2016–17

CHAPTER TWELVE

POSTSCRIPT

Writing in *The Times* of London in August 1985, the late Enoch Powell (at the time, the Unionist MP for South Down and author of the notorious 'Rivers of Blood' speech in 1968, dismissed *Across a Roaring Hill*. The book was, Powell protested, one in a line of work 'much petted and encouraged by those, in Great Britain and elsewhere, who want to bully the Northern Ireland electorate out of their settled conviction to remain within the United Kingdom'. How that collection of literary essays, 'exploring the Protestant imagination in Modern Ireland' (as the subtitle had it) could 'bully' an entire 'electorate' never failed to baffle me.

All these years later and here we are again, as historical landfall issues of frontiers and electorates' wishes abound. This time, though, the idea of a 'protestant' imagination is not quite so contentious as it was back in the 1980s' post-hunger strikes when the Troubles were agonisingly tearing the heart out of civic society. Reflecting upon these matters, Connal Parr in *Inventing the Myth: Political Passions and the*

Ulster Protestant Imagination has produced a timely and scholarly monograph on (primarily) playwrights whose backgrounds are generally and deeply influenced by their Protestant upbringing in 'Ulster', the Six Counties or Northern Ireland: Thomas Carnduff, St John Ervine, John Hewitt, Sam Thompson, Stewart Parker (the last two of whom died tragically in mid-career in their late forties), Ron Hutchinson, Graham Reid, Gary Mitchell, Marie Jones and Christina Reid, who sadly died in 2015.

Alongside the writing and beliefs of these writers, Parr has interwoven a cultural history of theatre in both parts of the island in exploring the role of The Abbey Theatre, and its Peacock stage in providing a platform for Northern Irish writers, Belfast's Lyric Theatre, and crucially the pioneering work of Charabanc Theatre Company, established in 1983, comprising 'Marie Jones, Eleanor Methven, Carol Scanlon, Brenda Winter, and Maureen McAuley' and Pam Brighton who, according to Parr, was introduced to the group by Belfast playwright Martin Lynch, a contemporary touchstone for Parr's study.

But also, and critically, Parr identifies the left-leaning social democratic views (with historical links to the Northern Ireland Labour Party) which many of the playwrights, such as Sam Thompson (who stood in the general election of 1964 for the NILP in the unlikely setting of South Down). It is this account which has, Parr suggests, been either kept out of the picture, patronised or simply derided: for Northern Protestantism (as if it were all the one thing) read bigotry and sectarian bile.

If Parr has achieved nothing else in his study, correcting this sloppy self-serving cultural prejudice would be enough. But *Inventing the Myth* goes much further. Drawing on extensive interviews Parr conducted and archive material, he has assembled irrefutable and substantiated proof that places the varieties of Northern Protestantism within the radical traditions of an inherited British working-class socialism of solidarity and its inherited social democratic beliefs in the separation of church and state, educational opportunities for all irrespective of class or creed, and the protection of the welfare state as of right.

Parr's study also reveals how many of his selected writers viewed Ireland, north and south, in much wider contexts of European political traditions. The tragedy, as we now know, is that these beliefs were not able to withstand the descent into political violence which characterised Northern society from the late 1960s until the late 1990s; a descent charted with great sympathy and dramatic irony in, for instance, Parker's *Pentecost*, set during the height of the unionist opposition to the Sunningdale Agreement in 1974 but also reveals the significant personal bravery given the danger Gary Mitchell's plays brought to both himself and his family. Several of the writers Parr discusses paid for their commitments to this democratic vision in lost opportunities and local opposition; others found little in the emerging Irish Free State to recommend it. St John Ervine's view of the Northern premier Lord Craigavon, of whom he wrote a biography, brought forth the ire of G.B. Shaw, who queried how Ervine could spend time researching 'that walking monument of obdurate mindlessness. Not even a reactionary, for reaction means movement and he was immovable.'

This anatomy of Northern literary culture brings into focus a society long since cut adrift from its industrial and social roots, something we are all being made aware of globally in the Trumpean western world in particular and in a fashion unforeseeable in the immediate years after the Good Friday Agreement was signed in 1998. In the two decades since, as Parr reveals, the 'deterioration' is not only in Protestant working-class neighbourhoods and produces the statistic: 'Northern Ireland's highest levels of unemployment and deprivation are to be found in the Catholic areas of Whiterock, the Falls, and the New Lodge in Belfast'. And continues: 'Forty-three per cent of children in West Belfast live in poverty against 21 per cent in East Belfast, while the highest levels of recorded crime are to be found – by far – in the same vicinities.' This is an appalling indictment of political leadership.

In exploring the social and political contexts of Northern Irish Protestantism, its inheritance of dissent – what Dawn Purvis, former leader of the Progressive Unionist Party refers to as 'independent thought' – and linking this history to the literary imagination and its 'connection to the theatre', Parr has opened the door on a little-appreciated strand in the history of creative self-questioning and honest critical debate all too often passed by in present-day Ireland.

Indeed, it might well be hard to credit today but when I left Belfast for Galway in 1974 there was a

sense of entering the faraway and unknown. Belfast
Protestants were pretty thin on the ground there so far
as I could tell; indeed, the only other fellow Northerner
I was aware of at UCG (now NUIG) when I got my
bearings was James Fairley, the botanist. Having a pint
in the wonderful Tavern bar in Eyre Square – alas,
long gone – one of the younger members of staff at
the College raised a few eyebrows when he remarked
somewhat theatrically that I had brought the Troubles
with me. Difficult as it is to recall those days of the
early 1970s it's even harder to believe that British
Army officers were still to be seen locally for a year or
so 'on leave'.

Religion rarely raised its head because so much
of the landscape – by which I mean *everything* from
school and hospital, college and public buildings
– was suffused with the ethos and symbols of the
Catholic Church. And there was also the *sound* of the
Angelus, along with the religious ceremonies that were
still marked then, such as Corpus Christi, with public
parades through the inner city of Galway where I lived
in a tiny network of high but narrow streets skirting
the Corrib River, and the canal ways and bridges.

I was not too put out by all of this, being, as Glenn
Patterson has called it, 'a lapsed Protestant'. Galway
could have been Genoa as far as I was concerned.
In fact, there was a tidy wee bar by that very name
only a few steps away from the flat in which I had
pitched up.

But as the decade developed and I started to realise
that this was going to be my home for some time

to come, I did notice how one *could* be offended by the unconscious assumption that being from Belfast, and having 'Gerald' as your first name, meant that you had to be, of course, Catholic. If and when this misunderstanding was clarified, nothing more was said. There was never a hint of spitefulness. Not a sectarian word – not among those who became my friends and eventually family. Not a bit of it. Sometimes a jest; occasionally a curious enquiry ('I always thought Protestants ...'), but that was it. I spent many hours in the famous Castle Hotel in Abbeygate Street discussing politics, as Aran men and women swept in and out, or in The Cellar Bar and Taaffe's, another haunt for Sunday-night revels, when traditional music flowed.

After I published a couple of books of poetry with what were considered at the time 'political' connotations – *The Lundys Letter* (1985) and *Sunday School* (1991) – and started to write critically about Protestantism and Irish culture – for instance, in *Across a Roaring Hill: Essays on the Protestant Imagination* – things changed a little, though not on the personal or local front.

It really is a long time ago. But some of the difficulties, the misconceptions and the strains resurfaced reading this wonderful and highly recommended collection of essays, *Protestant and Irish*, edited with diligent care by Ian d'Alton and Ida Milne, both of whom contribute valuable essays as well as setting the book in motion with a sensible introduction, 'Content and Context', which in turn, follows Roy Foster's Preface, 'The Protestant Accent', more on which anon.

The collection gives such rich and enveloping insight into the ways and manners by which *southern* Irish Protestantism adjusted to Irish independence from the 1920s to, roughly, the 1960s. If I had one reservation it is that the Northern part of the story could well have complemented the narratives included here, by which I mean the experience of those *from* the North who experienced life as Protestants *in* the 'Free State' (and eventual Republic) during the same timeframe. That might have produced an interesting perspective. The sense of a partitioned history should not really feature though, understandably, the pedagogies and practicalities of publishing have very much their own priorities.

This one minor caveat aside, *Protestant and Irish* is a necessary and timely volume. So much lived experience is contained within the book that it's difficult to know where to start in responding to the range and fascinating detail of the witness given by so many ordinary 'Prods' to what it was like growing up in different parts of the twenty-six counties. Many of the essays are based around oral histories, of interviews, some of which disclosed 'a reticence ... indicative of a legacy of hurt and resentment' particularly regarding the transgressive nature of 'mixed marriages' leading in some painful cases to the ostracising of family members. There are also some smart readings of southern-based cartoonists whose work included satirical portraits of upper-class Protestant society in *The Freeman's Journal* in the 1920s and *Dublin Opinion* in the 1930s. As

Caleb Richardson remarks in his consideration of the humourist and journalist, Patrick Campbell, 'humour played an important role in [Protestant]adaptation to life in independent Ireland, although not quite in the ways that one might think'.

From Protestants who were involved with the GAA, as recounted by Ida Milne, to those throughout the countryside engaged with local and national politics – as Tony Varley describes, sometimes against the current such as Robert Malachy Burke's standing for the Labour Party in Galway during the 1930s and '40s, facing a campaign of 'whispering and vilification' against him – to the Protestant republicans involved in revolutionary movements for independence and after, presented in great detail by Martin Maguire, the range and cultural mix of Irish Protestants is much more complex than generally believed.

But how was this community within a community viewed? According to the editors, the Irish 'government was relatively sensitive to its minority, more or less leaving it to its own devices. But the corollary was a subterranean exclusion.' Clearly, class background and locale were important in determining the wider Catholic society's understanding of those from a different religious background. None more so than in Dublin's 'Pockets of the Protestant working class' (the world out of which Sean O'Casey emerged) and 'the coterie of domestic servants in the south city, county and township areas and beyond or the skilled working-class Protestants in the suburb of Inchicore, with its railway works'. It is suggested that throughout the immediate period after the establishment of the Free State (1922), and as late as the 1950s, the protocol for dealing with religious and cultural differences was simple: 'deliberate amnesia on both sides ... it was neither necessary, nor important to remember ... Nevertheless, there is still within some elements of the Protestant community homage to a sensitivity to a presumed memory of murder, persecution and flight; whether real or imagined is beside the point.' (15) Other researchers such as Robin Bury, *Buried Lives: The Protestants of Southern Ireland* (2017), paint a different, gloomier story of decline, detachment and depression, tones that have attracted several important Irish writers to the fate of the minority as a narrative of emblematic status for modern societies, post-conflict and crisis.

Trinity College Dublin features throughout *Protestant and Irish* as its identification with the British imperial state and cosmopolitan culture comes increasingly under strain in the new emerging state. 'Change was certainly underway and was making an impact on the younger generation,' Miriam Moffitt declares in a fascinating re-run of 'Protestant Identity and the "State Prayers" Controversy, 1948–9':

> Trinity College, a bastion of unionism, was initially suspicious of the new state but moved towards an accommodation over time, which intensified after it negotiated a much-needed government

> grant in 1947. Some students realised as early as the 1920s that they were not bound by their parents' attitudes and that their Protestantism was not necessarily synonymous with loyalism, so the average student in the mid-1940s adopted a form of moderate nationalism: Ireland first and then the Commonwealth. (72)

This accords fairly closely with my own experience of several much older scholars and Fellows I met in the College in the 1980s, many of whom would have been young academics in the late 1940s and '50s and who eventually faded away as a younger generation pushed through important interior changes of both heart and mind in the 1960s and '70s, when TCD became an Irish college yet drawing upon its 400-year-plus history. Which brings me back to Roy Foster's preface 'The Protestant Accent' and his conclusion that while it 'may have vanished, independent Ireland was characterised by a Protestant intonation, and was all the richer for it'. It may well be that the 'accent' will alter somewhat over the next generation and that a Northern influence of independent thought plays an increasingly more progressive role in the mentalité of the Republic, post-Brexit. (Who can tell but unquestionably, at the present, the North seems to be lying well behind the Republic in terms of civic rights.) As the editors remark: 'There is another volume to be written about southern Protestantism in the turbulent years shaped by the Northern Irish conflict, economic boom-and-bust and the Weberian "protestantisation" of Irish Catholic society.'

Notwithstanding the assumption that 'strongly held conceptions of identity can neither be discarded nor disregarded', what *Protestant and Irish* proves is that the legacy of cultural Protestantism is only now, in the seventieth anniversary of the declaration of an Irish republic, finding its level in a cultural discourse that does not presume (as it once did) that to discuss such things is itself sectarian. How all this will impact upon the situation of Northern Ireland is another story altogether. It might be instructive to meditate upon how Irish society treated one of its largest minorities as a template for how other minorities will be facilitated in a post-Brexit Ireland, north and south.

In his Afterword 'Ireland's Mysterious Minority – a French-Irish Comparison', Joseph Ruane, looking at how the French Revolution 'put in place a new citizenship-based understanding of the French nation, undoing the *ancien régime*'s equivalence of Catholicity and Frenchness', suggests that with the notion of reunification – which 'could happen a long time from now, or it could come quicker than anyone imagines' – 'a historic opportunity to once again play a role in the politics of the island' awaits the Protestant minority, although 'Doing so would mean breaking with their low-key approach and asserting themselves in public debate'. As far as I can see, this opportunity would mean a new direction, a new deal and, most emphatically, a New Ireland in which the Protestant communities of the entire island, north and south, had ownership of how they and their future generations would find a place for their differing senses of cultural and religious difference and not simply as an unwanted and awkward add-on. That would be a big mistake.

2017–19

References

James Atlas, biographer of Delmore Schwartz and Saul Bellow, remarked in his wonderful book on the biographer's art, *The Shadow in the Garden* (2017), that he 'didn't want to weigh down [the] book with the scholarly apparatus of page-by-page notes so [I] have provided citations for each chapter in the form of paragraphs listing the main sources'. I have decided to follow suit in *The Sound of the Shuttle*, so if any reader wishes to track back to original sources, these are identified below. The essays haven't been updated in the light of new developments but I have lightly edited the originals to remove some clumsy constructions. As always, I am indebted to Jonathan Williams, the eagle-eyed first reader, and to all those who published this material in the first place, my thanks and appreciation. A special word of thanks to Galway Johnson, Dickon Hall and Bryan Rutledge for providing *Linenscape* by Nevill Johnson for the book's front cover. Dates under the essay identify when it was first published; double dates refer to sections in composite essays and when they were first separately published.

Chapter One: False Faces

Ireland's Field Day (Notre Dame: University of Notre Dame Press, 1986). Eavan Boland, 'Poets and Pamphlets', *The Irish Times*, Weekend Section, 1 October 1983. Seamus Deane, 'Why Ireland Needs a Fifth Province', *Sunday Independent*, 22 January 1984, 15. Declan Kiberd, *Ireland's Field Day*. Richard Kearney, *Ireland's Field Day*. Damian Smyth, 'Totalising Imperative', *Fortnight*, 309 (September 1992). *The Field Day Anthology of Irish Writing: Vol. III*, ed. Seamus Deane (Derry: Field Day Publications, 1991). Michael Longley, 'An Outsider Searching for His Home', Interview with Eileen Battersby, *The Irish Times*, Weekend Section, 11 January 1992. Patrick Wright, *On Living in an Old Country* (London: Verso, 1985).

Chapter Two: Telling a Story

Edna Longley and Gerald Dawe, *Across a Roaring Hill: The Protestant Imagination in Modern Ireland* (Belfast: Blackstaff Press, 1985). W.J. McCormack, *Ascendancy and Tradition* (Oxford: Clarendon Press 1985). *The Diaries of Franz Kafka: 1910–23*, edited by Max Brod (Harmondsworth: Penguin, 1964). André Brink, *Mapmakers: Writing in a State of Siege* (London: Faber and Faber, 1983). Albert Camus, *Youthful Writings* (Harmondsworth, Middlesex: Penguin Books, 1980). Heinrich Böll, *The Clown* (London: Weidenfeld and Nicolson, 1965). Salman Rushdie, 'Outside the Whale', *Imaginary Homelands: Essays and Criticism 1891–1991* (London: Granta Books, 1991). Brian Friel, 'Field Day Five Years On',

Linen Hall Review , Vol. 2, No. 2 (Summer 1985). Joe McMinn, 'In Defence of Field Day: Talking Among the Ruins', *Fortnight*, 9 September 1985, No. 224. Seamus Deane, 'The Protestant Mind in Irish Writing', *The Irish Times*, Weekend Section, 14 September 1985. Christopher Hitchens, *Prepared for the Worst: Selected Essays and Minority Reports* (London: Chatto & Windus, 1988). Enoch Powell, 'Cultural Ballyaches', *The Times*, 15 August 1985. Peter Gay, *Freud, Jews and Other Germans* (Oxford: Oxford University Press, 1978). Terence Brown, *The Whole Protestant Community: The Making of a Historical Myth* (Derry: Field Day Theatre Co. Ltd, 1985).

Chapter Three: Armies of the Night
Joseph Brodsky, 'Catastrophes in the Air', *Less Than One* (Harmondsworth: Viking, 1986). David Beresford, *Ten Men Dead: The Story of the 1981 Irish Hunger Strike* (London: Grafton Books, 1987). W. B. Yeats, *The King's Threshold* in *The Collected Works of W. B. Yeats, Vol. II: The Plays* (Basingstoke: Palgrave, 2001). Mary McCarthy, *The Writing on the Wall and Other Literary Essays* (Harmondsworth: Penguin Books, 1973). Martin Dillon, *The Shankill Butchers: A Case of Mass Murder* (London: Arrow Books, 1989).

Chapter Four: Anecdotes over a Jar
Denis Donoghue, *Yeats* (London: Fontana/Collins, 1971); *We Irish: Essays on Irish Literature and Society* (Brighton: Harvester Press, 1986). Padraic Fiacc, *The Wearing of the Black* (Belfast: Blackstaff Press, 1974).

Edna Longley, *From Cathleen to Anorexia: The Breakdown of Irelands* (Dublin: Attic Press, 1990). Eavan Boland, *A Kind of Scar: The Woman Poet in a National Tradition* (Dublin: Attic Press, 1989). Richard Murphy, *The Price of Stone* (London: Faber and Faber, 1985). Richard Murphy, *The Mirror Wall* (Dublin: Wolfhound Press, 1989). Graham Hough, *The Dark Sun: A Study of D. H. Lawrence* (London: Gerald Duckworth, 1956, rep. 1970). Seamus Heaney, *The Government of the Tongue: The 1986 T. S. Eliot Memorial Lectures and Other Critical Writings* (London: Faber and Faber, 1988). Hannah Arendt, *Men in Dark Times* (New York: Harcourt, 1968).

Chapter Five: Our High Destiny
Thomas MacDonagh, *Literature in Ireland: Studies Irish and Anglo-Irish* (Dublin: Talbot Press, 1916). Pier Paolo Pasolini, *The Lutheran Letters* (Manchester: Carcanet New Press, 1983). Václav Havel, 'Letter to Dr. Gustav Husak', 'An Anatomy of Reticence', *Living in Truth* (London: Faber and Faber, 1987).

Chapter Six: The Sound of the Shuttle
Richard Rowley, *City Songs and Others* (London: Duckworth, 1918). John Keats, *Letters of John Keats* (London: University of London Press, 1963). *The Oxford Literary Guide to the British Isles*, eds. Dorothy Eagle and Hilary Carnell (Oxford: Clarendon Press, 1977). Geoffrey Bell, *The Protestants of Ulster* (London: Pluto Press, 1978). F. S. L. Lyons, *Culture and Anarchy in Ireland 1890–1939* (Oxford: Clarendon

Press, 1979). John Wilson Foster, *Forces and Themes in Ulster Fiction* (Dublin: Gill and Macmillan, 1974). John Keats, 'The Fall of Hyperion', *John Keats: The Major Works* (Oxford: Oxford University Press, 1990). A. T. Q. Stewart, *The Ulster Crisis: Resistance to Home Rule (1912–1914)* (London: Faber and Faber, 1967). A. T. Q. Stewart, *Edward Carson* (Dublin: Gill and Macmillan, 1981). W. B. Yeats, 'September 1913', *Yeats's Poems*, ed. A. Norman Jeffares (Basingstoke: Palgrave, 1996). David Millar, *Queen's Rebels: Ulster Loyalism in Historical Perspective* (Dublin: Gill and Macmillan, 1978). Derek Mahon, 'Nostalgias', 'Ecclesiastes', *Poems 1962–1978* (Oxford University Press, 1979).

Chapter Seven: A Kind of Country

Ronan Bennet, 'An Irish Answer', *The Guardian*, 16 July 1994. Gerald Dawe, 'The Aunt's Story', *Heart of Hearts* (Loughcrew: The Gallery Press, 1991). Neal Ascherson, *Games with Shadows* (London: Radius, 1988). David Gervais, *Literary Englands: Versions of 'Englishness' in Modern Writing* (Cambridge: Cambridge University Press, 1993).

Chapter Eight: What's the Story?

Declan Kiberd, 'Celtic Nationalism and Postcoloniality', *SPAN*, 41(October 1995). Robert Crawford, *Devolving English Literature* (Oxford: Clarendon Press, 1992). Terence Brown, *SPAN* 41 (October 1995). Terry Eagleton, 'The Ideology of Irish Studies', unpublished text of lecture, *Eighth Desmond Greaves Summer School* (1996). Samuel Beckett, *Disjecta*

(London: John Calder, 1983). Hugh Kearney, *The British Isles: A History of Four Nations* (Cambridge: Cambridge University Press, 1989). Caryl Phillips (ed.), *Extravagant Strangers: A Literature of Belonging* (London: Faber and Faber, 1997). W. B. Yeats, *Autobiographies* (London: Macmillan, 1955/1980). Graham Greene, *The Third Man* (Harmondsworth, Middlesex: Penguin Books, 1971).

Chapter Nine: Cultural Resolution
Samuel Beckett, 'The Calmative', *The Complete Short Prose 1929–1989* (New York: Grove Press, 1995).

Chapter Ten: Unhealthy Intersections
Eavan Boland, 'Poets and Pamphlets', *The Irish Times*, Weekend Section, 1 October 1983. Samuel Beckett, 31 January 1938, *The Collected Letters: Vol. 1* (Cambridge: Cambridge University Press, 2009). Fintan O'Toole, 'Preservation of self is true measure of elite's genius', *The Irish Times*, 26 April 2011. John McGahern, *Love of the World: Essays* (London: Faber and Faber, 2009). Patrick Kavanagh, *Self Portrait* (Dublin: Dolmen Press, 1975). Conor Cruise O'Brien, 'An Unhealthy Intersection', *New Review*, 2, no. 16 (July 1975). Louis MacNeice, *Modern Poetry: A Personal Essay* (Oxford: Clarendon Press, 1968). Helen Lewis, *A Time to Speak* (Belfast: Blackstaff Press, 1992).

Chapter Eleven: The Hand of History
Adrian Barlow, *English after Brexit* (Leicester: English Association, 2016). Simon Grimble, *Brexit and the*

Democratic Intellect (https://readdurhamenglish. wordpress.com/2017/05/16/brexit-and-the-democratic-intellect/). George Orwell, 'Politics and the English Language', *Essays of George Orwell* (London: Everyman, 2002). Dennis Kennedy, 'British Politicians can still prevent Brexit', *The Irish Times*, 3 January 2017.

Chapter Twelve: Postscript
Edna Longley and Gerald Dawe, *Across a Roaring Hill: The Protestant Imagination in Modern Ireland* (Belfast: Blackstaff Press, 1985). Connal Parr, *Inventing the Myth: Political Passions and the Ulster Protestant Imagination* (Oxford: Oxford University Press, 2017). Glenn Patterson, *Lapsed Protestant* (Dublin: New Island Books, 2006). Ian d'Alton and Ida Milne (eds), *Protestant and Irish: The Minority's Search for Place in Independent Ireland* (Cork: Cork University Press, 2019). Robin Bury, *Buried Lives: the Protestants of Southern Ireland* (Dublin: History Press, 2017).